9423 / 251 / 7⁵⁰

HANDICRAFT SERIES.

A Series of Practical Manuals.

Edited by PAUL N. HASLUCK, Editor of "Work."

Price 50cts. each, post paid.

House Decoration. Comprising WHITEWASHING, PAPERHANGING, PAINTING, etc. With 79 Engravings and Diagrams.
Contents.—Colour and Paints. Pigments, Oils, Driers, Varnishes, etc. Tools used by Painters. How to Mix Oil Paints. Distemper or Tempera Painting. Whitewashing and Decorating a Ceiling. Painting a Room. Papering a Room. Embellishment of Walls and Ceilings.

Boot Making and Mending. Including REPAIRING, LASTING, and FINISHING. With 179 Engravings and Diagrams.
Contents.—Repairing Heels and Half-Soling. Patching Boots and Shoes. Re-Welting and Re-Soling. Boot Making. Lasting the Upper. Sewing and Stitching. Making the Heel. Knifing and Finishing. Making Riveted Boots and Shoes.

How to Write Signs, Tickets, and Posters. With 170 Engravings and Diagrams.
Contents.—The Formation of Letters, Stops, and Numerals. The Sign-writer's Outfit. Making Signboards and Laying Ground Colours. The Simpler Forms of Lettering. Shaded and Fancy Lettering. Painting a Signboard. Ticket-Writing. Poster-Painting. Lettering with Gold, etc.

Wood Finishing. Comprising STAINING, VARNISHING, and POLISHING. With Engravings and Diagrams.
Contents.—Processes of Finishing Wood. Processes of Staining Wood. French Polishing. Fillers for Wood and Filling In. Bodying In and Spiriting Off. Glazing and Wax Finishing. Oil Polishing and Dry Shining. Re-polishing and Reviving. Hard Stopping or Beaumontage. Treatment of Floors Stains. Processes of Varnishing Wood Varnishes. Re-polishing Shop Fronts.

Dynamos and Electric Motors. With 142 Engravings and Diagrams
Contents.—Introduction. Siemens Dynamo. Gramme Dynamo. Manchester Dynamo. Simplex Dynamo. Calculating the Size and Amount of Wire for Small Dynamos. Ailments of Small Dynamo Electric Machines : their Causes and Cures. Small Electro-motors without Castings. How to Determine the Direction of Rotation of a Motor. How to Make a Shuttle-Armature Motor. Undertype 50-Watt Dynamo. Manchester Type 440-Watt Dynamo.

Cycle Building and Repairing. With 142 Engravings and Diagrams.
Contents.—Introductory, and Tools Used. How to Build a Front Driver. Building a Rear-driving Safety. Building Tandem Safeties. Building Front-driver Tricycle. Building a Hand Tricycle. Brazing. How to Make and Fit Gear Cases. Fittings and Accessories. Wheel Making. Tyres and Methods of Fixing them. Enamelling. Repairing.

Decorative Designs of All Ages for All Purposes. With 277 Engravings and Diagrams.
Contents.—Savage Ornament. Egyptian Ornament. Assyrian Ornament. Greek Ornament. Roman Ornament. Early Christian Ornament. Arabic Ornament. Celtic and Scandinavian Ornaments. Mediæval Ornament. Renascence and Modern Ornaments. Chinese Ornament. Persian Ornament. Indian Ornament. Japanese Ornament.

Mounting and Framing Pictures. With 240 Engravings, etc.
Contents.—Making Picture Frames. Notes on Art Frames. Picture Frame Cramps. Making Oxford Frames. Gilding Picture Frames. Methods of Mounting Pictures. Making Photograph Frames. Frames covered with Plush and Cork. Hanging and Packing Pictures.

Smiths' Work. With 211 Engravings and Diagrams.
Contents.—Forges and Appliances. Hand Tools. Drawing Down and Up-setting. Welding and Punching. Conditions of Work ; Principles of Formation. Bending and Ring Making. Miscellaneous Examples of Forged Work. Cranks, Model Work, and Die Forging. Home-made Forges. The Manipulation of Steel at the Forge. (Continued on next page.)

DAVID McKAY, Publisher, 610 South Washington Square, Philadelphia.

Glass Working by Heat and Abrasion. With 300 Engravings and Diagrams.

Contents.—Appliances used in Glass Blowing. Manipulating Glass Tubing. Blowing Bulbs and Flasks. Jointing Tubes to Bulbs forming Thistle Funnels, etc. Blowing and Etching Glass Fancy Articles; Embossing and Gilding Flat Surfaces. Utilising Broken Glass Apparatus; Boring Holes in, and Riveting Glass. Hand-working of Telescope Specula. Turning, Chipping, and Grinding Glass. The Manufacture of Glass.

Building Model Boats. With 168 Engravings and Diagrams.

Contents.—Building Model Yachts. Rigging and Sailing Model Yachts. Making and Fitting Simple Model Boats. Building a Model Atlantic Liner. Vertical Engine for a Model Launch. Model Launch Engine with Reversing Gear. Making a Show Case for a Model Boat.

Electric Bells, How to Make and Fit Them. With 162 Engravings and Diagrams.

Contents.—The Electric Current and the Laws that Govern it. Current Conductors used in Electric-Bell Work. Wiring for Electric Bells. Elaborated Systems of Wiring; Burglar Alarms. Batteries for Electric Bells. The Construction of Electric Bells, Pushes, and Switches. Indicators for Electric-Bell Systems.

Bamboo Work. With 177 Engravings and Diagrams.

Contents.—Bamboo; Its Sources and Uses. How to Work Bamboo. Bamboo Tables. Bamboo Chairs and Seats. Bamboo Bedroom Furniture. Bamboo Hall Racks and Stands. Bamboo Music Racks. Bamboo Cabinets and Bookcases. Bamboo Window Blinds. Miscellaneous Articles of Bamboo. Bamboo Mail Cart.

Taxidermy. With 108 Engravings and Diagrams.

Contents.—Skinning Birds. Stuffing and Mounting Birds. Skinning and Stuffing Mammals. Mounting Animals' Horned Heads; Polishing and Mounting Horns. Skinning, Stuffing, and Casting Fish. Preserving, Cleaning, and Dyeing Skins. Preserving Insects, and Birds' Eggs. Cases for Mounting Specimens.

Tailoring. With 180 Engravings and Diagrams.

Contents.—Tailors' Requisites and Methods of Stitching. Simple Repairs and Pressing. Relining, Repocketing, and Recollaring. How to Cut and Make Trousers. How to Cut and Make Vests. Cutting and Making Lounge and Reefer Jackets. Cutting and Making Morning and Frock Coats.

Photographic Cameras and Accessories. Comprising How to MAKE CAMERAS, DARK SLIDES, SHUTTERS, and STANDS. With 160 Illustrations.

Contents.—Photographic Lenses and How to Test them. Modern Half-plate Cameras. Hand and Pocket Cameras. Ferrotype Cameras. Stereoscopic Cameras. Enlarging Cameras. Dark Slides. Cinematograph Management.

Optical Lanterns. Comprising THE CONSTRUCTION AND MANAGEMENT OF OPTICAL LANTERNS AND THE MAKING OF SLIDES. With 160 Illustrations.

Contents.—Single Lanterns. Dissolving View Lanterns. Illuminant for Optical Lanterns. Optical Lantern Accessories. Conducting a Limelight Lantern Exhibition. Experiments with Optical Lanterns. Painting Lantern Slides. Photographic Lantern Slides. Mechanical Lantern Slides. Cinematograph Management.

Engraving Metals. With Numerous Illustrations.

Contents.—Introduction and Terms used. Engravers' Tools and their Uses. Elementary Exercises in Engraving. Engraving Plate and Precious Metals. Engraving Monograms. Transfer Processes of Engraving Metals. Engraving Name Plates. Engraving Coffin Plates. Engraving Steel Plates. Chasing and Embossing Metals. Etching Metals.

Basket Work. With 189 Illustrations.

Contents.—Tools and Materials. Simple Baskets. Grocer's Square Baskets. Round Baskets. Oval Baskets. Flat Fruit Baskets. Wicker Elbow Chairs. Basket Bottle-casings. Doctors' and Chemists' Baskets. Fancy Basket Work. Sussex Trug Basket. Miscellaneous Basket Work. Index

DAVID McKAY, Publisher, 610 South Washington Square, Philadelphia.

HANDICRAFT SERIES (continued).

Bookbinding. With 125 Engravings and Diagrams.
Contents.—Bookbinders' Appliances. Folding Printed Book Sheets. Beating and Sewing. Rounding, Backing, and Cover Cutting. Cutting Book Edges. Covering Books. Cloth-bound Books, Pamphlets, etc. Account Books, Ledgers, etc. Coloring, Sprinkling, and Marbling Book Edges. Marbling Book Papers. Gilding Book Edges. Sprinkling and Tree Marbling Book Covers. Lettering, Gilding, and Finishing Book Covers. Index.

Bent Iron Work. Including ELEMENTARY ART METAL WORK. With 269 Engravings and Diagrams.
Contents.—Tools and Materials. Bending and Working Strip Iron. Simple Exercises in Bent Iron. Floral Ornaments for Bent Iron Work. Candlesticks. Hall Lanterns. Screens, Grilles, etc. Table Lamps. Suspended Lamps and Flower Bowls. Photograph Frames. Newspaper Rack. Floor Lamps. Miscellaneous Examples. Index.

Photography. With 70 Engravings and Diagrams.
Contents.—The Camera and its Accessories. The Studio and Darkroom. Plates. Exposure. Developing and Fixing Negatives. Intensification and Reduction of Negatives. Portraiture and Picture Composition. Flashlight Photography. Retouching Negatives. Processes of Printing from Negatives. Mounting and Finishing Prints. Copying and Enlarging. Stereoscopic Photography. Ferrotype Photography. Index.

Upholstery. With 162 Engravings and Diagrams.
Contents.—Upholsterers' Materials. Upholsterers' Tools and Appliances. Webbing, Springing, Stuffing, and Tufting. Making Seat Cushions and Squabs. Upholstering an Easy Chair. Upholstering Couches and Sofas. Upholstering Footstools, Fenderettes, etc. Miscellaneous Upholstery. Mattress Making and Repairing. Fancy Upholstery. Renovating and Repairing Upholstered Furniture. Planning and Laying Carpets and Linoleum. Index.

Leather Working. With 152 Engravings and Diagrams.
Contents.—Qualities and Varieties of Leather. Strap Cutting and Making. Letter Cases and Writing Pads. Hair Brush and Collar Cases. Hat Cases. Banjo and Mandoline Cases. Bags. Portmanteaux and Travelling Trunks. Knapsacks and Satchels. Leather Ornamentation. Footballs. Dyeing Leather. Miscellaneous Examples of Leather Work. Index.

Harness Making. With 197 Engravings and Diagrams.
Contents.—Harness Makers' Tools. Harness Makers' Materials. Simple Exercises in Stitching. Looping. Cart Harness. Cart Collars. Cart Saddles. Fore Gear and Leader Harness. Plough Harness. Bits, Spurs, Stirrups, and Harness Furniture. Van and Cab Harness. Index.

Saddlery. With 99 Engravings and Diagrams.
Contents.—Gentleman's Riding Saddle. Panel for Gentleman's Saddle. Ladies' Side Saddles. Children's Saddles or Pilches. Saddle Cruppers, Breast-plates, and other Accessories. Riding Bridles. Breaking-down Tackle Head Collars. Horse Clothing. Knee-caps and Miscellaneous Articles. Repairing Harness and Saddlery. Re-lining Collars and Saddles. Riding and Driving Whips. Superior Set of Gig Harness. Index.

Knotting and Splicing, Ropes and Cordage. With 208 Engravings and Diagrams.
Contents.—Introduction. Rope Formation. Simple and Useful Knots. Eye Knots, Hitches and Bends. Ring Knots and Rope Shortenings. Ties and Lashings. Fancy Knots. Rope Splicing. Working Cordage. Hammock Making. Lashings and Ties for Scaffolding. Splicing and Socketing Wire Ropes. Index.

Beehives and Beekeepers' Appliances. With 155 Engravings and Diagrams.
Contents.—Introduction. A Bar-Frame Beehive. Temporary Beehive. Tiering Bar-Frame Beehive. The "W. B. C." Beehive. Furnishing and Stocking a Beehive. Observatory Beehive for Permanent Use. Observatory Beehive for Temporary Use. Inspection Case for Beehives. Hive for Rearing Queen Bees. Super-Clearers. Bee Smoker. Honey Extractors. Wax Extractors. Beekeepers' Miscellaneous Appliances. Index.

DAVID McKAY, Publisher, 610 South Washington Square, Philadelphia.

" WORK" HANDBOOKS.

WOOD FINISHING

WOOD FINISHING

COMPRISING

STAINING, VARNISHING, AND POLISHING

WITH ENGRAVINGS AND DIAGRAMS

EDITED BY

PAUL N. HASLUCK

EDITOR OF "WORK" AND "BUILDING WORLD"
AUTHOR OF "HANDYBOOKS FOR HANDICRAFTS," ETC. ETC.

PHILADELPHIA

DAVID McKAY, Publisher

610, SOUTH WASHINGTON SQUARE

1906

PREFACE.

THIS Handbook contains, in a form convenient for
everyday use, a comprehensive digest of the knowledge
of Staining, Varnishing, and Polishing Woods,
scattered over ten thousand columns of WORK—one
of the weekly journals it is my fortune to edit—and
supplies concise information on the general principles
of the crafts on which it treats.

In preparing for publication in book form the mass
of relevant matter contained in the volumes of WORK,
much that was tautological in character had to be
rejected. The remainder necessarily had to be arranged
anew, altered and largely re-written. From these
causes the contributions of many are so blended that
the writings of individuals cannot be distinguished for
acknowledgment.

Readers who may desire additional information re-
specting special details of the matters dealt with in this
Handbook, or instruction on kindred subjects, should
address a question to WORK, so that it may be
answered in the columns of that journal.

P. N. HASLUCK.

La Belle Sauvage, London

CONTENTS.

LIST OF ILLUSTRATIONS.

———◦◇◦———

WOOD FINISHING.

CHAPTER I.

By French polishing and spirit varnishing, or both in cómbination, household furniture and many other things are covered with a lac solution, with the object of giving them a polished mirror-like surface, showing the beauty and figure of woods to the best advantage. By painting, the latter qualities are hidden, and to an extent the cabinet-maker's skill has been so much labour in vain. The surface, as it comes from the cabinet-maker's hands, shows an unfinished article, to which dust and finger-marks would soon give a dirty appearance.

Staining is the process of imparting to the surface of wood a colour different from its natural one. Staining requires no preliminary preparation, the stain being applied directly to the wood. Most stains raise the grain of the wood to a considerable extent, so before applying varnish, it is necessary to sand-paper the wood enough to render the grain smooth again ; this sometimes involves the use of a second coat of stain, after which the sand-paper must be again applied. To simply stain a piece of wood in a uniform tint, and to produce a gloss by coats of varnish, is not all that is required in these modern days of keen competition ; and this is particularly true in the case of furniture of the medium and higher grades.

The method of finishing most suitable for woodwork depends on circumstances. For coarse work varnish does very well, but for articles of furniture French polishing is to be preferred, as finer results can be obtained by it. In addition to these methods, we have oil and wax polishing processes, which are to be preferred for some kinds of work, and which are treated on in a later chapter.

Choice articles of furniture, from the substantial sideboard to the flimsy fretwork ornament, may be varnished instead of polished ; but such a well-finished surface cannot be got with the simpler and easier process, which is also more expeditious. To distinguish that which will be worth polishing properly, and that for which a coat of varnish is sufficient, must be left to the reader's consideration, but he will get better results from careful varnishing than from badly executed polishing ; though the simple wax polishing described on p. 50 can be done by anybody who has patience.

Furniture made from pine may be considered the only kind which it is proper to varnish, though even this is sometimes French polished. However, unless particularly well made and finished, it is not customary to polish it. Its appearance is improved by polishing, like that of other woods ; but as the chief advantage in pine furniture is its cheapness, varnishing is supposed to be good enough for it. The process of japanning, by which much of the cheaper kinds of pine furniture is finished, is similar to painting. This handbook will be confined to processes in which the grain or natural figure of the wood is simply brought out and improved by a transparent covering. Mahogany, walnut, and all the finer woods used in making furniture should be polished, in order to make them look their best. The novice must form his own opinion as to when he ought to finish by polishing and when by varnishing.

A glossy surface on wood is often described indifferently as varnish or polish, and to a certain extent rightly so. An expert has no difficulty in distinguishing the mode of finishing which has been adopted for a piece of woodwork, but it is not easy to explain the distinction. He would not confound the two terms, polish

and varnish ; but if asked to point out the difference
he would probably say in effect that varnish is laid
on with a brush, while French polish is applied by
means of a rubber, an explanation which will bear
supplementing.   In order to arrive at a clearer idea of
the difference between the two processes, it will be well
to understand the action of a varnish.

Varnish is applied in a liquid state, and this liquid is
a solvent for the gum or resin used.   The surface of the
work is coated with the varnish.   The solvent evaporates,
leaving a film of the resin which was dissolved in it.
Wood, or anything else so treated, is said to be
varnished.

The medium used to obtain a French polished surface,
although really only a varnish, is one of a much finer
kind than is generally suggested by that word.   French
polish might be described as a special varnish for French
polishing.   However, both the finished gloss and the
material by means of which the gloss is produced are
commonly spoken of as French polish.   The material
is thin varnish, which experience has shown to be most
suitable for producing a fine, smooth, glossy surface by
the French mode of polishing.

In the furniture trade the cabinet maker, the
upholsterer, and the polisher are distinct persons,
each often totally unfamiliar with any branch of the
business beyond his own special one.   But is there any
sound reason for this being the case ?   The furniture-
trade artisan who is able to do polishing and all that
appertains to it will command a better market for his
labour than he who ignores everything outside his
particular groove.   This applies more especially to those
in country districts, but even in the larger centres of
population facility in more than one branch of a trade
cannot fail to be of advantage.

The celebrated Vernis Martin (which means simply
Martin's Varnish) produced a very fine finished surface
by means of some material or manipulation which the
inventor kept a secret, and which is said to have died

with him. This, however, seems improbable, for it is reasonable to suppose that his success induced others in the same line of business to imitate, and the result is French polish. This present-day French polish is Vernis Martin as nearly as we know how to imitate it. Martin's materials, and his mode of producing the gloss or polish, were, probably, different from ours; but he made his reputation by the somewhat cumbersome processes of smoothing or polishing a varnish; but the simpler process now known as French polishing is sufficient for practical purposes, and only those prompted by curiosity will care to try a more tedious way of getting similar effects. At the same time, it must not be assumed that there is no more progress to be made in the art of wood-polishing.

The polisher of to-day is called upon to do many difficult jobs. It is not enough for him to be able to put a clear bright polish on anything that may be brought to him. He must be able to match the various coloured woods, giving to the whole an appearance of carefully-selected and joined veneers. Here a knowledge of how to use chemicals, stains, and dyed polishes must be brought into use. Some parts may require to be made darker, dark parts may have to be made lighter, or oak may have to be treated so as to present an appearance of age.

The unvarnished and unpainted oak fittings of stables have been noticed to change from their light colour to a rich brown. Observant minds have traced this result to ammoniacal fumes. Acting on this principle, many oak articles are given an appearance of age, or enriched in colour, by shutting them up for a time in a cupboard or air-tight box on the bottom of which has been placed an open dish of liquor ammonia. Failing a suitable cupboard in which to do this, chemistry comes to our aid, and we get a like result by wiping over with a solution of bichromate of potash, common soda, or lime-water. With careful management, and by the aid of these and dyed polishes, common bay wood or plain mahogany can be made to look equal to Spanish mahogany.

The coloured stringings or inlays, with their many-coloured woods, found round work-boxes and on writing-desks, are not all real. The polisher and the chemist have played their respective parts. And there are musical-boxes, etc., with imitation pearl inlays and stringing, which is simply bird's-eye maple dyed green, verdigris and vinegar being mostly used for this. Again, flowers, birds, etc., may be painted on the panels of doors; or failing ability to paint, it is possible to get transfers that look exceedingly well when polished over; or birds, flowers, and such-like may be cut out from thin paper, and fastened to the work with thin polish or varnish, giving them, when dry, a coat of white, hard varnish, which can be polished, after first sizing the pictures with isinglass.

Polishing partakes a good deal of the nature of an art. Skill is necessary to make a good polisher, as well as knowledge about the materials and their manipulation, and this skill, of course, is only to be acquired with practice. Some people regard French polishing as a mystery, rather than an art to be acquired. When the novice tries to do the work himself the refusal of the polish or gloss to come up under his hands is indeed mysterious. French polishing looks such easy, almost lazy, work (albeit, somewhat tending to dirty the hands) that the baffled novice may be pardoned for thinking he has got hold of the wrong stuff, or that he has been misdirected, and though either of these circumstances may be the cause of failure, it is much more likely to be owing to want of skill. Possibly the foregoing remarks may have a discouraging effect on the novice, but everything will be done in these pages to remove difficulties and to indicate right methods of working. The rest will depend upon himself.

The beginner, however clever he may be, must not expect to finish his work as well as those who have had years of experience, and he need not be discouraged if his first attempts do not reach his expectations. The instructions in this handbook will at least explain to beginners what they ought to do, and it is hoped that even the more advanced will find in it suggestions which will lead to increased skill.

CHAPTER II.

PROCESSES OF STAINING WOOD.

STAINING may be said to be divided into three classes : —(a) The staining of deal or common woods to match the better class, such as ebony, walnut, rosewood, mahogany, etc. (b) The darkening of natural wood to imitate a superior class : as, for example, common oak to match brown or pollard oak, common baywood to match best mahogany. (c) Decorative work, such as the imitation of inlaid woods, etc.

Some persons, who lay claim to good taste, strongly object to staining wood on the ground that it gives an appearance that is not natural. All painted woodwork has the natural beauty of the woods entirely covered. In all bare woodwork staining has probably played an important part in the decorative treatment. Even wood of the finest quality that money can buy, no matter how carefully selected and joined, will be treated when it passes through the French polisher's hands with some staining medium, in the form of red oil, coloured "filling-in," dyed polish, varnish, or stain, to bring out the beauty of the woods and to show the cabinet-maker's handiwork to the best advantage. When veneers are used in furniture manufacture, the chances that stain is used are doubled. In modern marquetry or inlaid work it will be found that the woods employed are not all real. The old exponents of marquetry have left excellent specimens, in which only three kinds of wood are used ; but the range of colours and shading as now used is much greater.

Many persons prefer to use the commoner kinds of wood in the manufacture of their household furniture, and by staining these to imitate closely the more

expensive woods. This chapter is written chiefly for
the benefit of such people. It is recommended that
those stains which, though useful enough in their way,
require acids or chemical and special apparatus, should
be avoided, as the same end can be gained by other and
simpler means.

There are two methods of staining :—(a) Surface-
staining, in which, as the name implies, the staining is
effected by compounds, in the nature of pigments, laid
upon the surface like paint, and forming a thick opaque
coating, which does not, to any considerable degree, penetrate the fibre of the wood. (b) Body-staining, in which
the stain is usually applied as a thin wash, which, enter-
ing the pores of the wood, colours it to some little depth
below the surface. To make stains penetrate very
deeply into wood is neither an expeditious nor a simple
process to those unaccustomed to the work. For ordinary purposes, body-staining is quite sufficient.

There are many stains, made both in liquid and in
powder. Most of these are cheap and reliable. One
gallon of liquid stain will cover a hundred square yards ;
and after buying a small sample bottle and finding it
suitable, one can rely upon getting a further supply to
match. This is not always so with home-made stains.
Stains in powder are more convenient for carrying.
The only solvent needed is water, so they are easy to use,
and valuable for stencilling and decorative purposes.

It is not for furniture alone that these stains may
be used ; no reason appears against their more extensive
use for interior decoration in preference to painting
and graining. Suppose a floor margin is to be stained,
and it is desired to have a pattern of a darker shade
around the inner edge, as shown in the illustrations
which appear on page 78. It is easy to take up a
little powder stain and mix with water to the consistency of thin paint, and apply by means of a stencil-
plate and brush, as would be done with distemper. In
order to show up stained work to the best advantage,
the woodwork is required to be of superior class and

free from sap; this is an extra expense in the first instance. On the other hand, it is less expensive to keep the wood fresh and clean when stained than it would be to apply successive coats of paint, then grain and varnish.

Dealers sell combined stains and varnish as a means of simplifying the process. One material will often do duty for shades varying from light oak to dark walnut, the light shade being gained by one coat, successive coats giving darker shades and, consequently, thicker surface, a process which cannot be commended. Although cheap and simple, these combined stains and varnishes cannot be recommended for hard wear. Being mixed in varnish, the stain does not penetrate the fibres of the wood to the same extent as when applied alone. When these combined stains and varnishes are used, the cheaper class should be avoided, as the soft, resinous varnish employed will readily show scratches and marks.

Most druggists sell aniline dyes in packets and in tubes which may be usefully employed on wood for self colours only—as distinct from various imitations of woods.

Their introduction has had a disastrous effect on the old vegetable-dye market. Orchella wood, madder, safflower, and turmeric, mentioned in old recipes, are now practically unsaleable, and dealers generally do not keep them in stock; nevertheless, vegetable stains are exceedingly useful.

Aniline dyes are of two kinds—one dissolves in water, the other in spirits; but they have a tendency to fade on exposure to light. To the former a little vinegar, which has the property of preventing this fading to a great extent, can be added. To mix aniline dyes with varnish, they must be dissolved in spirits—to use with a spirit-varnish or naphtha-varnish. They are only partially successful in oil-varnish or painters'-varnish. The quantity required to stain a pint of varnish must be a matter of experiment, as so much depends on the covering quality of the varnish, and whether

B

the tone required is to be got in one, two, or three applications.

Marquetry work can be very closely imitated by means of stains only, the stains used being purely vegetable. It is claimed that the stains are durable, and that they leave no smell or stickiness. Each bottle of stain, medium, preparing solution, and polish may be bought for about sixpence. Neat little boxes, containing seven stains and the three other requisites, are also prepared, and sold for about five shillings. The colours employed include walnut, mahogany, ebony, green, red, yellow, rosewood, satinwood, grey, olive, blue, and crimson.

The large number of colours that can be obtained from dye woods, which include logwood, red sanders, madder, fustic, orchella wood, safflower, sandal wood, Socotrine aloes, Barbadoes aloes, and nut-galls, is worth noticing.

Many are to be obtained from common plants growing in abundance almost everywhere. The well-known blueberry, when boiled down with a little alum and a solution of copperas, will develop an excellent blue colour; treated in the same manner with a solution of nut-galls, it produces a dark brown tint; with alum, verdigris, and sal-ammoniac, various shades of purple and red can be obtained from it. The fruit of the elderberry, so frequently used for colouring spirits, will also produce a blue colour when treated with alum. The privet boiled in a solution of salt, furnishes a serviceable colour, and the over-ripe berries yield a serviceable red. The seeds of the common spindle tree, when treated with sal-ammoniac, produce a beautiful purplered. The bark of the currant-bush, treated with a solution of alum, produces a brown. Yellow is obtained from the bark of the apple-tree, the box, the ash, the buckthorn, the poplar, the elm, etc., when boiled in water and treated with alum. A lively green is furnished by the broom corn.

The art of marquetry wood-staining offers scope for

the display of artistic designs and for the development
of the purely manual faculties, and its suitability for
amateurs is becoming generally known. The requisite
apparatus is neither large nor costly; the work can
be made effective, and generally novel; and any kind
of wood may be utilised, though holly, sycamore, and
lime are the best varieties.

CHAPTER III.

FRENCH POLISHING.

VARNISHING can be done by any person with little or no practice, and is suitable for common articles of furniture ; but French polishing cannot be done successfully without considerable practice, though when skilfully managed it enhances the beauty of most woods. The beginner should not attempt to polish any article of value before he has gained experience by practising upon unimportant articles.

Although it may be said that each kind of timber requires different treatment, the general manipulation is very similar for all. The ingredients of the various polishing preparations are generally few and simple, and success does not necessarily lie in complication and multiplicity of mixtures. In the main, French polishing consists in coating the wood with a thin film of shellac, either pure or mixed with other gums and resins, and then getting on that film a gloss as brilliant and durable as possible.

Generally, the wood has to be prepared and various minor details attended to before this can be done. For example, the pores of open grained wood must be stopped or, as the process is generally called, filled, to get a smooth surface and to prevent excessive absorption of the liquid polish. Then the appearance of some woods is improved and enriched by oiling them before applying the polish. This oiling, to a certain extent, darkens and mellows them, and brings up the figure.

The temperature and atmosphere of the place in which French polishing is done are of considerable importance. Work cannot be done properly in a cold or damp room, as then the polish will get chilled, and as it sets on the wood become opaque and cloudy. To avoid this the polisher should work in a warm room. The temperature for a living room, about 70°, is about that suited for polishing. In warm summer weather a fire is not necessary, but in winter it is. If the polisher notices that his polish chills, he must increase the heat of his room. If a moderate amount of warmth be brought near the surface as soon as any chill is observed it will probably disappear. A small article may be taken to the fire, but with large work this course would hardly be convenient. In such cases a good plan is to hold something warm a short distance from the chilled surface, but on no account must it touch, nor must the heat be great enough to scorch the polish. A common plan, but not altogether a good one, is to hold a piece of burning paper near the chill. An ordinary flat iron is very useful for small chilled patches. When the article is cold or damp, chill is more likely to occur. It is, therefore, always necessary to make sure after a stain has been used that the wood has become thoroughly dry.

Not less important is the employment of suitable materials, both in the polish and in the tools of the polisher's art. These latter consist almost entirely of wadding or cotton wool and soft linen or cotton rags, from which the rubbers to apply the polish are made ; and a few bottles are wanted to hold the various polishes, stains, and their components.

The pad with which French polish is applied is called the rubber. Without it the French polisher can do little in actual polishing, although he may not require it in the preliminary operations of oiling and staining. However simple in itself the rubber may be, it should be properly and carefully made of suitable materials ; otherwise good work cannot be done with it. Those who have seen polishers at work may be inclined to infer that no great care is necessary, for a dirty rag covering an equally uninviting lump of wadding is usually seen. Examination will show the rubber to be more carefully made than might have been expected, and the expert polisher would probably prefer it to a

nice clean-looking rubber such as a novice would
choose. Nevertheless, a dirty rubber is not wanted,
for dirt is fatal to first-class work; hence the polisher
should keep his rubbers scrupulously clean. They will
naturally get stained and discoloured with the polish,
but that is a very different matter from being dirty.
Old rubbers are preferable to new ones, provided they
have been properly taken care of and not allowed to
get hard.

For flat surfaces or fretwork a wad may be prepared
by using a strip of torn woollen cloth from 1 in. to 2 in.
wide. Cloth with a cut edge is not recommended for
this purpose, as it is too harsh. Roll the strip very
tightly into a wad about 1 in., 2 in., or 3 in. diameter,
according to the size of the work, and tie tightly round
with fine twine (Fig. 1). This will give as nearly as
possible a rubber resembling Fig. 2. This wad is put
into a double thickness of linen cloth, and the ends
are gathered up like the ends of a pudding-cloth; they
are not tied, but are grasped as a hand-piece while being
used. This form of rubber would, however, be useless
for bodying up mouldings, beads, quirks, moulded
hand-rails, newel posts, etc., and when polishing large
mahogany doors or other framed furniture it would be
impossible to get well into the corners of sunk panels,
as in Fig. 3.

A well-shaped, soft, pliable rubber, with its rag
covering free from creases, is to a practical French
polisher equivalent to a sharp, finely-set, smoothing
plane in the hands of a cabinet maker. The form in
general use is shown in Fig. 4. With such a rubber
made of wadding, one is enabled to get into corners,
round turned work, and up to the edges of mouldings
in a manner impossible with a hard, round rubber. To
make it, take a sheet of wadding—this is 9 in. wide—
and tear off a piece 6 in. long; this will form a con-
veniently-sized rubber, suitable for most work; but for
small work use one of smaller size. Double the wadding,
making it 6 in. by $4\frac{1}{2}$ in. Squeeze this in the hand,

keeping the skin unbroken, till in shape it nearly resembles half a pear ; the illustrations, Figs. 4, 5, 6,

Fig. 1.—Side View of Rubber for French Polishing.

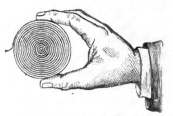

Fig. 2.—Face of Roll used for French Polishing.

Fig. 3.—Rubber used in Corner of Framed Panel.

show what is meant and the method of holding it. The rubber should then be charged with polish, and covered with a piece of clean, soft rag. In folding the rag, twist it on the upper side of the rubber. Each additional twist will bring it to a sharper point and cause the polish to ooze through its surface. It is not necessary to put a rag covering on the rubbers first used. The rubber must be kept free from creases, otherwise it will cause the surface to which it is applied to be stringy or full of ridges.

Though rags have been mentioned as suitable for the outer covering or casing of the pad, some care in their selection is necessary. A piece with a seam across it

Fig. 4.—Usual form of   Fig. 5.—Form of Rubber for
Rubber for French Polishing.   getting into Corners.

Fig. 6.—Method of holding the Rubber when in use.

would never do for a rubber; and anything which would tend to scratch the film of polish as it is being laid or worked on in the final operation of spiriting off must be carefully avoided. They may be either cotton or linen, and ought to be perfectly soft and fine, or, at any rate, free from knots or lumps. Some polishers advise the exclusive use of linen, but this is a needless restriction. It may be mentioned that new material may be used as well as rags. To render this suitable, all traces of the sizing and stiffening with which it may have been finished must be removed by a thorough washing.

Any material to be used for a polishing rubber must be thoroughly well dried. Indeed, the necessity of avoiding damp cannot be too much insisted on. With regard to the substance of the rubber, white wadding is the best to use, and this is readily obtainable from any upholsterer or chemist. It may be purer if got from the latter, but it is certainly much dearer than any reasonable upholsterer would charge for something equally suitable. Wadding bought from an upholsterer has a thin skin on one or both sides, according to whether it has been split or not. This skin must be removed, leaving nothing but the soft cotton. For a few pence enough ought to be obtainable to last a considerable time. It may be useful to know that, if it is clean, the raw material used in cotton manufacturing districts will do as well as the finest wadding. Cotton flock, used by upholsterers as a stuffing for mattresses, chairs, etc., is not suitable for polishing, except perhaps for the coarsest work. Even for this it should not be used if anything better is available. Rubbers composed entirely of flannel are occasionally recommended for special kinds of work. It is doubtful if there is any advantage in using flannel, except for large flat surfaces, which can be got over more quickly with a large rubber than with a small one. The novice is advised to use the wadding rubber, and to become an expert polisher with it before experimenting with anything else.

The size of the rubber will, to some extent, depend on the nature of the work, but that above given may be regarded as generally suitable. A very large rubber is not advisable at first, and the polisher, as he gains experience, must be guided by circumstances. In handling it, moreover, the polisher will be equally guided; a rubber of moderate dimensions is usually held by the tips of the thumb and fingers, but the polisher will probably find a large rubber can be more conveniently used by holding it in the palm of the hand.

The rubber must be charged with polish for use,

and some care will have to be exercised in doing this. The covering of the rubber is opened so that a little polish can be dropped on the wadding. A convenient way of doing this is to have the polish in a bottle, the cork of which has a channel or notch cut in it to allow only a few drops to escape at a time. Some polishers dip a portion of the rubber into the polish, but the other method is more generally adopted. It must not be saturated; only enough polish to moisten the wadding must be used, or what will appear through the rag covering when pressed. The rubber having been thus 'charged, gather up the edges of rag as before directed. Then, to distribute the polish equally, press the rubber moderately firmly into the palm of the other hand. The rubber ought now to be ready for application to the wood, which may be assumed to have been properly prepared to receive its first coating of polish.

At this stage the principal thing is to get a good body of polish evenly spread on the wood. How this may best be done depends on circumstances; but if the desired result is obtained, the precise method is of secondary consequence. Let it be assumed that the work to be done is a small flat surface. With moderate pressure on the rubber, quickly wipe over the entire surface, first with the grain of the wood, then across it. Then without delay go over it more minutely, the motion generally adopted for the rubber being shown in the illustration on p. 38 (Fig. 7). At first the pressure should be gentle, but it should be increased as the polish gets worked in and the rubber drier, though at no time must the rubbing decline to scrubbing.

While the rubber is in contact with the wood it must be kept constantly in motion. An important point is not to allow the rubber to remain stationary on the woodwork during temporary absence or at the end of the day's work. As the rubber gets dry it must be recharged with polish, but let the novice beware of using this in excess.

Old rubbers are better than new, so when done with they should be kept in an air-tight receptacle, such as a tin canister or a biscuit box. When any job is finished, do not throw the rubber away under the impression that a rubber once laid aside becomes useless. This occurs only when it is left exposed to the air, because the spirit evaporates, leaving the shellac to harden. If laid aside for a length of time the rubbers will become hard, even when kept in a box, unless it be perfectly air tight, which it probably will not be. A few drops of spirit put into the box now and then will, however, keep the contents in proper condition for use.

CHAPTER IV.

FILLERS FOR WOOD AND FILLING IN.

FILLERS are used by French polishers for much the same reason that size is used before varnishing—viz. to prevent immoderate absorption of the polish by the wood. French polish, or even thicker varnish, when applied to wood, sinks in or is absorbed in places, instead of remaining on the surface in a uniform coat. Here and there it will be observed that the polish or varnish has given more gloss than elsewhere. Where the gloss is brightest the varnish has sunk least.

The grain may be filled up by going over the wood with polish till the pores are closed, and some beginners may want to know why anything else in the nature of a filler should be used. The reason is that comparatively valuable French polish need not be used when a cheaper material serves the purpose, the use of which also saves time. Woods that are open in the grain and porous specially need a filler, while fine close-grained woods do not, and may be polished without. Still, a suitable filler can do no harm to any kind of wood, however fine the grain may be, so there can be no disadvantage in going over it with one preparatory to polishing. Though it may be a slight waste of time, a preliminary rub over with polish suffices when working on a fine wood, such as olive, which is both close and hard. To attain the desired thin glossy film of shellac, which shall not be liable to grow dull unreasonably soon, the woods ordinarily used in furniture—ash, oak, mahogany, walnut, etc.—should have the grain filled, for they are all of comparatively open grain ; ash and oak being especially coarse, are called by polishers "hungry woods." Polishers usually give such woods one or more coats of spirit varnish as an aid to filling up the grain.

Before commencing the process of filling-in,

thoroughly brush all dust out of the grain of the wood, for this is wood-dust, glass from the glass-paper, and dirt —all inimical to grain lustre if mixed up with the grain stopper.

For filling a cheap class of work, many polishers content themselves with giving the work one or two coats of glue or patent size, heavily stained by the addition of some dry pigment. For mahogany finish add Venetian red till it gives quite a red tinge; for walnut add brown umber; for pine, add yellow ochre. Apply the size hot with a brush, and rub it in lightly with a piece of rag, finishing the way of the grain, and taking care in the case of turned or moulded work to get the filler well in the recessed parts. Of course, work that has been sized will not need filling in.

As many different kinds of fillers are used, and each has its advocates, it will be advisable to name the principal fillers used in the trade, and to make a few remarks about each, so that learners can experiment with them, and perhaps finally fix on that which may seem to suit best. All will be found reliable, for good work is turned out by polishers with any of them, and even an extremely prejudiced individual would hesitate to say that any one is really bad, though he uses only that which suits him best. Sometimes, owing to the price, he uses the easiest and quickest, irrespective of its quality.

Wood fillers ready for use are made for most kinds of wood, and, as a rule, they require only thinning with a little turpentine. When it is desired to make a filler instead of purchasing one ready made, proceed as follows: Take a portion of either china clay or cornflour; add boiled linseed oil, and stir until the mixture is of the consistency of putty. Then add patent dryers and thin with turpentine. If the wood on which the filler is to be used is to be kept light in colour, use raw oil and the lightest variety of dryer.

Apply the filler with a pound brush, rubbing it well into the pores of the wood. Allow it to remain on for, say, half an hour, and then proceed to remove all of it from the surface. Rub off as much as possible with shavings, or wood wool, and with a pick, made of a piece of wood sharpened at the end, remove the superfluous filler from the carvings, mouldings, and corners. Mouldings having sharp edges or lines, such as sunken beads, are best treated with a short-haired brush, such as a housemaid's scrubbing-brush. Remember that the object is to remove as much of the filler as possible, because if any be left on the surface it will show up in dark spots when the work is finished. It will, of course, be understood that the filler must be properly tinted to produce the colour required, and to accord with the stain. The pigments to be used for producing certain effects will be referred to in another chapter.

The filler to be mentioned next is varnish, or extra thick polish, which is rubbed into the wood till the pores are full. This is a clean and natural filler, but it is a troublesome one, and the results are not better than those arrived at by a cheaper and more expeditious method. Occasionally it may be an advantage to use this, though for trade purposes and at trade prices on ordinary furniture the polisher is out of pocket by employing it. This process of filling is rubbing in polish or thin varnish, and when it is dry smoothing down with fine glass-paper. The application of polish and paper must alternate till the former no longer sinks, and this will depend on the nature of the wood and on the filler used. The process will be completed much sooner with a fine, close-grained, hard wood than with a coarse open grained one, such as ash.

Brown hard varnish and polish mixed form a fair preliminary application, but they do not tend to a good surface at the finish, so are suitable for common work only. The proportions are two-thirds polish and one-third varnish (brown or white hard); the mixture is put on carefully and quickly with a brush. It must not be brushed, but must be let alone till hard.

Whiting and turpentine can be recommended for a good general filler. The filler is both clean and economical, does not raise the grain as when water is used, and contains no grease; it is, therefore, not open to the objections which are urged against other fillers, and in the hands of inexperienced polishers it is, perhaps, the most likely to ensure a successful result. An advantage it possesses over plaster-of-Paris and water is that it does not harden quickly; some urge that it does not harden sufficiently, but this objection cannot be treated seriously. Use finely-crushed whiting, and mix to the consistency of thick paint, but still thin enough to be worked into the wood. Take up a little at a time on coarse rag or canvas, and rub well in crossways of the grain, the work having previously been wiped over with raw linseed oil; apply equally all over the article to be polished. Wipe off clean and set aside a few hours or overnight to enable the filling to set, though, if necessary, polishing may be proceeded with at once.

Direct filling with polish is modified by the use of fine pumice-powder, which renders the process quicker and better. This method is more practised in France than in this country; here it is sometimes employed by the trade, but it has not been generally adopted. It requires some experience to use it with advantage, but apart from the time required, it is doubtful if a better means of filling the grain has been discovered, for it is both clean and free from greasiness. Polish is the basis of this filler, the pumice-powder being useful in assisting to fill by getting into the pores of the wood as well as in rubbing down inequalities of the polish. The powder is kept in a muslin bag, and lightly sprinkled on the wood, which is then gone over with an ordinary rubber fairly charged with polish. Only a small quantity of the pumice-powder should be used at a time, or the work suffers. Instead of sprinkling the powder on the wood, some polishers prefer to put it on the sole of the rubber. Whatever method be adopted the work will require papering down afterwards, but perhaps not to the same extent as when no pumice-powder has been used.

The object of pumice-powder is twofold : First, as in coach painting, for levelling-down purposes, and to bring up the lustre of the varnish by giving a dead under-surface on which to apply it ; secondly, for use on spirit varnish or French polished surfaces for dulling purposes, thus giving what is known on antique furniture as egg-shell finish, or that semi-lustrous finish largely practised in the United States on American organs.

A very much used filler is composed of Russian tallow, mixed with either plaster-of-Paris or whiting. The chief thing in its favour is that it is a quick process, and therefore allows of polishing being done at a comparatively small cost of labour ; but tallow is not a nice material to work with. The tallow and plaster are made into a stiff paste and well rubbed into the wood, from which any excess must be wiped off. Any fillers that set hard must be wiped off while they are still soft. Apart from its unpleasantness in working, tallow is apt to increase the tendency of the polished wood to sweat, through the grease breaking through the film of lac. Oil or grease, in connection with polish, can only be regarded as a necessary evil. There are fillers which do not contain grease, and it is just as well to use them, even if it be admitted that a tallow filler is not prejudicial to good work or to durability.

Beyond wiping over with an oily rag, to bring out the figure and tone of the wood, the less oil is used the better for permanency of lustre, as oil forms no part of polish in itself, being used only as a vehicle to work the gums easily. The true secret of laying a polish that shall bear future inspection lies in using the oil so that it shall always be on the top of the polish—not underneath ; and the final point is to remove this oil in finishing.

Since grease is objectionable, it may be asked whether water cannot be used instead, to render the plaster or whiting soft and pasty. It often is; but the objection is that water is apt to raise the grain of the wood, which means making it rough, whilst the tallow does not raise the wood at all. The rough surface can be rubbed smooth with glass-paper. Whiting, or plaster-of-Paris and water, can certainly be used as a filler, and this mixture is preferable to those in which tallow or grease is found.

As tallow is unpleasant stuff, many polishers discard it in favour of raw linseed oil, mixed with some polish. The use of this with whiting overcomes the objection to water; but this is not altogether a suitable filler for the novice. With too much oil, sweating is apt to occur some time; while with too little oil in the mixture, the filling is apt to remain on the surface instead of being forced into the pores of the wood. It is not possible to give the proportions of oil and polish which shall be suitable to all occasions, so the polisher must use his own discretion, and he may as well leave this filler alone till he has acquired experience; but in experienced hands it is a really good one.

A little plaster and polish, without the oil, make a good filler, but it must be rubbed in, and *all* the superfluous filler removed with fine glass-paper before using pure polish.

A good filler for oak and ash is water and methylated spirits and plaster-of-Paris. It should be prepared and used in the following manner:—Crush · the plaster-of-Paris into a fine powder, and place in a saucer or other open vessel; in another put the spirits. Then take a piece of soft rag, and soak in the spirits; then dip in the plaster, rub hard into the wood, and clean off. Do not mix the plaster and spirits together in a paste, like the ordinary filling. A preliminary rub with polish before filling in will keep the grain smooth, and stop the sweating to a great extent, as there would be a foundation of polish.

It is advisable that white fillers should be tinted to correspond with the colour of the wood on which they

c

are used. The polisher will seldom have occasion to use
in his fillers any colours other than the following : for
mahogany, rose-pink ; for walnut, or any brown wood,
such as stained oak, Vandyke brown or umber ; and for
ebonised work, gas-black is as good as any.   Light
woods, of course, may have any white filler applied ;
but if it should be deemed advisable to tint it, there
will be no difficulty in doing so, as an exact match is not
necessary.

In addition to these ordinary fillers, common to the
British workshop, there are several patent and American
fillers; but none of them has come into general use,
nor seems likely to supersede the commoner varieties.
A complaint against them is that they are more
expensive, without having sufficient compensating
advantages.

CHAPTER V.

BODYING IN AND SPIRITING OFF.

THE term bodying, applied to the polisher's art, means coating the wood with a thin, evenly-distributed layer of the polish. The way in which this is done greatly affects the appearance and the durability of the gloss. When the body is too thin, the gloss subsequently given to it may at first be beautiful, but as the polish sinks or perishes the gloss fades. When the body is too thick the gloss may appear all right, but the work is apt to look treacly, as though varnish had been used; besides, a thick body impairs the pure tone of some woods. The high degree of excellence to which polishing is capable of being brought is seen only on the best cabinet work. Polish on second-rate furniture is generally in keeping with the inferior quality of the woodwork. The cheap gaudy furniture which is often seen in shops must not be taken as models of polishing. The price paid for polishing is reduced, with the result that inferior polish is used and less time is spent on the work. Although the best materials and the expenditure of time and labour will not ensure good work by unpractised hands, they are important factors, and it will be wise to use materials of good quality.

To make a good average polish, neither too thick nor too thin, about six ounces of shellac to each pint of methylated spirit will be required, but great exactitude in the proportions is not necessary. The proportions may vary according to the fancy of the polisher, and, to some extent, according to the nature of the work he is engaged on. If the polish turns out too thick, it can be thinned by adding more spirit; if too thin, the deficiency can be made up by adding more shellac. A rough-and-ready way of measuring the proportions is

to half fill a bottle with the roughly-broken shellac, and
then fill up with ordinary methylated spirit.

The shellac dissolves gradually, and the process is
hastened by an occasional shaking or stirring with a
stick. Heat is not necessary; indeed, the preparation
of polish by heat is dangerous.

Two kinds of polish are used. One, known as
"white polish," is nearly colourless; the other is known
as "brown polish," or simply "polish." The latter is
always understood if unqualified by the word "white."
White polish is made with white or bleached shellac;
the other with ordinary orange or reddish-brown shellac.

Either polish may be used on any kind of wood,
except where great purity of tint is required. The
white is to be preferred for all light woods, such as light
oak, ash, sycamore, satin, etc., while the brown may be
used on darker; but even on these, white polish is
good, with the exception of mahogany, the only ordinary
furniture wood for which a decided preference might be
given to brown polish. Under ordinary circumstances,
however, either polish may be used indiscriminately.
The point as to brown or white polish for dark wood
belongs to the higher branches of the polisher's art.

It will be seen that white polish is the more generally
useful of the two, so those who do not care to keep both
kinds may confine themselves to it. Through the
slightly higher price of the bleached shellac, it costs
a little more, but the extra cost is so small that it is
hardly worth considering by those who use small
quantities. Those who use polish in large quantities
can have both kinds.

Polish bought ready made may be equal to that made
at home from the recipe given, for there is nothing to
prevent manufacturers using the same ingredients, and
many of them do. Still, from the impossibility of
knowing the ingredients in ready-made polish, there is
some risk attending its use. From the price at which
some polish is sold, it is fair to suppose that something
cheaper than spirit or shellac has been used; and

though good polish may be bought, it is better for the user to prepare his own, which can be depended on. Bought polish may be thoroughly good in every way —brilliant, clear, and durable—but those who are best able to judge generally prefer to make their own polish to do the best class of work. Prejudice may account for this preference.

Manufacturers of polish assert that, in addition to shellac, certain gums or resins improve the quality of the polish, when used with knowledge and discretion For instance, one gum may give increased elasticity, while another may harden the film; but for a good all-round polish, which can be relied on, many polishers assert that there is nothing to surpass a simple solution of shellac and methylated spirit. A few approved formulæ for polishes are given at the end of this book, so that those who feel inclined to do so may experiment for themselves. Shellac is the principal ingredient in nearly all. Those persons who cannot polish with shellac and spirit alone will not be able to do any better with the more complicated mixtures; therefore, no one should remain under the impression that he will do better if he works with another kind of polish.

Enough having now been said about the material, we may proceed to the using of it for bodying. In the first place, the wood must be prepared by filling of one kind or another, as fully explained in Chapter IV., and rubbed down smoothly with fine or worn glass-paper, in order to make it fit to receive the polish, for a high degree of finish cannot be got on a rough surface. The rubber, which consists of cotton wadding with a soft rag cover, with which the polish is applied, has been sufficiently treated on in Chapter III., so that nothing more need be said about it. Work, rubber, polish, and a little raw linseed oil being ready, bodying in may be proceeded with in the following way :—

Moisten the wadding with polish; put the rag cover on carefully, so that it is without folds or wrinkles. Dab the rubber into the palm of the left hand **to**

distribute the polish evenly, and cause it to moisten the
rag at the bottom properly.   Supposing the work is
a panel or flat surface, the following will be found a
good method of treating it, and it is one that is
followed more or less closely by experienced polishers :—

Rub briskly across the grain, to get the surface
covered with polish ; then by a series of circular move-
ments, as shown by the lines in Fig. 7, go over the
whole of the work.   A moderate pressure should be
applied, which should be increased gradually as the

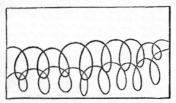

Fig. 7.—The Path of the Rubber in French Polishing.

rubber dries, but the movement should at no time
degenerate into mere scrubbing.   In order that the
rubber may work smoothly without sticking, a little
of the raw linseed oil should be applied.   The less of
this used the better, and if it can be dispensed with
altogether no harm will be done.   To make the rubber
work smoothly a very little will suffice ; the tip of a
finger, moistened with oil, and touched on the face of
the rubber is all that is required.   The rubber
must not be dipped in the oil, nor must the oil
be dropped on it from a bottle ; for by these means
more oil would be applied than is necessary, and this
would prove fatal to good work.

The only recognised oil used in French polishing is
raw linseed.   This may be worked over the natural woods
in the first place, to give them that peculiar tone that
cannot be gained by other means, otherwise the less oil

used the better for the durability of the work. Bear in
mind that it forms no part of polish in itself, being used
only to enable us to work the gums easily ; thus, without its aid the polish rubber would be apt to stick or
drag, thus breaking up the surface instead of levelling
it. On any surface in which spirit varnish forms a part
this will be particularly noticeable ; and in any case,
it is next to impossible to get that beautiful level surface gained by spiriting out unless a little oil is used.

As the rubber dries, more polish must be applied to
it, as was done in the first instance, with more oil as
required. A small quantity of polish goes a long way,
and the novice must carefully avoid making the rubber
wet. It should be no more than fairly moist.

Many a beginner, noticing how tedious the work is
with a dry rubber, may think that if he used more
polish the desired result would be more quickly attained.
If the object were merely to get the wood coated, this
might be the case ; but the result of using too much
polish would be that the shellac left by the quick
evaporation of the spirit would be ridgy and irregular,
instead of in a fine, even coating or body. Anything
approaching a flow of polish from the rubber must be
avoided. When the rubber is not sufficiently charged
with polish, the labour of bodying up will be unduly
protracted, or may be rendered impossible if no polish
can be rubbed on to the wood.

The first bodying-in process should be continued till
it seems that the wood absorbs no more of the polish.
There will be a perceptible gloss on its surface, but it
will be streaky, and the rubber-marks will show very
distinctly. All these marks will be removed later on.
It may be thought that, if the polish is too thick or too
thin, the result will be very much the same as if the
rubber were too wet or too dry. The principal objection to having the polish too thin is that it will take
more time in working a good body on the wood.
It will, however, be better to risk this rather than to
have the polish too thick. An experienced polisher

would soon detect fault in either direction by the way in which the polish works, but the novice must be on the look-out for irregularities in the shape of lumps or ridges, and, with a little attention, he will have no difficulty in avoiding serious mishaps.

Let the work stand for at least a day, carefully covered up from dust; on examining it the body will be found to have altered in appearance to an extent which will depend upon how much the polish has sunk into the wood. The work must be again bodied up as before, always remembering to use as little oil as possible. Then it will be again laid aside, and the bodying process repeated till the polish no longer seems to sink in, even after the work has lain aside for a few days. When this stage is reached the bodying may be considered complete, and the work ready for the first polishing operations. Before proceeding to consider these, however, the novice will do well to note the following hints :—

The number of times the work will require to be bodied depends on circumstances. Fine, close-grained woods will not require so many as the more open kinds, such as oak, ash, mahogany, etc.; but for the best work, which is intended to be as durable as can be, it need rarely exceed four. An interval of one or more days may elapse between the successive bodies, the chief object of waiting being to let them sink as much as they will. If, after the work has been laid aside for a few days, the polish has not sunk at all, no advantage would be gained by giving it another body. It is very seldom that the first body is enough, but often only one body is applied, where either low price or limited time will not allow of more; so those who wish to do polishing need not think the process cannot be hurried.

Still, imperfect bodying is not advisable, as such work will soon want touching up. When work is made merely to sell, one body, and that of the slightest, is sufficient—from the seller's point of view, if not from the buyer's. Between the bodyings, especially after the first and second, the surface of the work should be rubbed down with fine glass-paper—not to rub the body off, but just enough to smooth the surface. It may here be remarked that pumice powder, used in moderation, is useful for working down inequalities of surface. Glass-papering has been recommended as necessary after the first and second bodies, but the process may be done after any others, though it should not be required if the work has been skilfully done. In fact, the final bodying up may be regarded almost as the beginning of the spiriting off.

Before beginning to work a fresh body on a previous one, it is as well to wash the surface gently with luke-warm water, not using too much of it, in order to remove the grease and allow the rubber to work freely. The water must be thoroughly dried up before applying the rubber. In moderation the washing can never do harm, and is, generally, an advantage, though not absolutely necessary. When a long interval has elapsed, the washing should never be omitted, as dust will settle on the work ; and it need scarcely be said that dust should not be rubbed into the polish.

When bodying up, polishers should see that their hands are clean and free from old polish, which is so often seen on them. If they are soiled with old polish or shellac, bits are apt to flake off and destroy the surface of new work. This may be an appropriate place to say that any polish which sticks to the hands may be washed away with hot water and soda, or with methylated spirit.

The body should be thin, as it is not so much the quantity of body on the wood as its quality that is important ; it is also essential that it should be applied with sufficient intervals between the successive bodies to allow of sinkage.

Another important matter is to dry the rubbers well by working them on each body till dry, and not to moisten them frequently. By this means the film of shellac is kept thin. Neither a wet nor a dry rubber should on any account be allowed to stand on a surface being polished. The rubber must be kept moving, and should glide gradually on to the work, not be dabbed down on it. In the initial stages of bodying, care in this respect is not so important as later on, when it is absolutely necessary. The same precaution should be used when lifting the rubber from the work.

For the guidance of beginners, it may be stated that if they take care of the edges of the work the rest of the surface will look after itself. The reason is that the edges are apt to be somewhat neglected, and the polish to be less there than elsewhere. The secret of a good durable polish depends primarily on a good body, and this, in its turn, on sufficient time having been allowed for sinkage.

The final operation in French polishing, by which the gloss is put on the body previously applied, is known as spiriting off. In this operation rubber marks and smears of all kinds are removed, and the beautiful surface, known as French polish, is the result. Bodying is important so far as durability is concerned, but spiriting is more so with regard to finish. If the worker fails in spiriting, his previous efforts will, to a great extent, have been in vain. Disregarding staining, darkening, and other processes, with which a good polisher should be acquainted, the spiriting is perhaps the most severe test of skill in the whole process of polishing; and a man who can manage this part of the work really well may be considered a competent polisher.

The first operation to be described in the process of spiriting off partakes very much of the nature of bodying in. At the beginning it is bodying, and at the end spiriting. The two processes merge one into the other. There is no abrupt break, as between filling and bodying, except for the intermediate stage, although the processes are well defined, both in character and purpose. This intermediate stage is not always practised, but it is recommended when good work is wanted. Briefly, spiriting off consists in washing the bodied surface with methylated spirit. This being understood, the final bodying up, or first spiriting off, whichever this process may be called, consists in gradually reducing the quantity of polish in the rubber, and supplying its place with spirit. The polish is gradually reduced by the addition of spirit till all the polish has been worked out of the rubber. The rubber may be charged, first with three parts polish and one part spirit; next time equal quantities; the third time three parts spirit and one part polish; and the fourth charging will be with spirit only. It does not follow that these proportions need be strictly observed, nor are they so in practice, but this example illustrates the process. The last rubber will be almost free from polish, and it should be worked till it is dry, or nearly so.

At this stage spiriting proper may begin, and a fresh rubber should be used. It need not be a new one, but it should be one which has been used only for spiriting, and which has no polish on it. It will be better if it has three or four coverings of rag on its face, which can be removed as they dry. If only one cover is used the spirit is apt to evaporate too quickly. The spirit in the rubber has a tendency to partially dissolve the shellac or body on the wood. This it does to a very limited extent, unless the rubber is made too wet, when there is danger of not only spiriting and smoothing the surface, but of actually washing away the body. This mishap must be carefully guarded against. There should be enough spirit to allow the surface of the body to be softened and smoothed, but no more, and the rubbing should be uniform, and not more in one place than in another. There is hardly any likelihood of the novice erring by using too little spirit, so he may be reminded that the less of it there is in the rubber at a time the better. The rubbing should be gentle at first, becoming harder as the spirit dries off, and oil must not be used on the rubber face, for when there is oil either on the rubber or on the work, the polish cannot be brought up.

The chief cause of failure lies in getting the spirit-rubber too wet, and so softening and tearing up the gums. Many meet with success by dispensing with it, using instead a swab of clean, soft rag, fairly damp (not wet) with methylated spirit.

If the spiriting-off process is being done correctly the gloss will soon begin to appear, and when it seems approaching a finished condition, the rubber ought to be moved only in the direction of the grain, and not across it nor with circular motion. The final touches should be given with the soft rubber rag alone, care being taken not to scratch the surface, which is now softened by the action of the spirit. The surface will gradually harden, but for a time it should be handled with care, and nothing be allowed to come in contact with it, or it is very likely to be marked. It should also be protected from dust, for any settling on it may be retained by the polish, the lustre of which would certainly suffer.

Cabinet-makers, and perhaps dealers in furniture, who do not keep an experienced polisher, or who may not be able to get their work done out, may be reminded that, circumstances permitting, polished furniture should be wiped over with a spirit-rubber an hour or two before it is sent home, to freshen it up. If the surface is at all soft, neither packing mats, nor anything else likely to injure it, should be allowed to come in contact with it. The polishing on many things sent long journeys is often greatly disfigured from mat and other markings, but they are easily touched up on arrival at their destination.

CHAPTER VI.

GLAZING AND WAX FINISHING.

GLAZING, though an imitation, has a recognised accept-
ance among polishers. It is remarkably convenient
occasionally, and in some cases possesses an advantage
over spiriting, so that it may fairly be classed among
the ordinary processes of polishing. When done in
moderation, glazing is as useful on furniture carving as
the application of spirit varnish. Such work is commonly said, and justly, to be French polished. The real
objection to glaze finish is that, though at first the
appearance is equal, it is not so durable as the other.
Glaze may be said to be even superior to badly-spirited
finish, and here is the chief claim it has for notice. It
is seldom that a casual polisher can manage to do
spiriting thoroughly, for the reason that he has not
sufficient opportunity of acquiring practice.

Nevertheless, finishing by means of glaze is not so
good as the method by spiriting, when the latter is well
done, and should be considered as a means of getting
the same effect easily and quickly—an imitation, in fact,
of the real thing; the difference between the spirit and
glaze finishes is that in the one case the effect is produced
by friction, in the other by the addition of a thin fine
varnish to the surface of the body of polish. In the
former case the polish itself is polished; in the latter it
is varnished with a mixture known commonly as glaze,
but to which other names are sometimes given.

Among polishers who command a fair price for their
work, glaze is of comparatively limited application, and
is confined to those parts where the spirit-rubber cannot
be conveniently used, or where its use is not necessary.
Instances of such may be found in chair-rails and
various parts of the frame. These are usually polished,

more or less, before the chair is upholstered, or, at any rate, before the outer covering is put on, the finishing being almost necessarily done last of all. The less the chair is handled by the polisher the better, especially if the covering is a delicate one, for there is less risk of injury with one or two wipes over with the glaze rubber than with the more prolonged spiriting.

Glaze may be used with advantage in inlaid work, where the inlay is slightly, though perhaps not intentionally, higher than the surrounding wood. In such a case it is better to resort to glaze than to finish with the spirit rubber. On fretwork, also, glaze may often be used with advantage, and, generally, it is unobjectionable on parts which are not subject to wear and tear. It will stand a moderate amount of handling, but not so much as good hard spirited-off polish, and the lustre is not so durable.

Glaze, under one or other of its different names, may be bought ready made, but for reasons similar to those given in connection with French polish, the home-made article is to be recommended. The preparation of glaze is simple, the ingredients being gum benzoin and methylated spirit. After the benzoin is dissolved, the solution should be strained through muslin to free it from foreign matter. The proportions may vary, but those given for polish do very well, and with the substitution of crushed benzoin for shellac the process of making is exactly the same.

Gum benzoin differs greatly in quality, but the best should be used by the polisher. Compared with lac it is expensive, so that the saving which is attributed to its use is mainly in time, which is money, at least from a trade point of view. Cheap benzoin is not to be relied on, and in a strange place an experienced polisher would look with suspicion on any offered at a very low price, however satisfactory its appearance. Where material is liable to adulteration, the best way to avoid imposition is to go to a reliable dealer and to pay a fair price.

Glaze, as used by French polishers, can be bought

ready made at most drysaltery stores, as patent glaze, at from 8s. to 16s. per gallon, according to quality and age; it improves with age. To make the genuine article, dissolve 6 or 8 ounces of best gum benzoin (costing 2s. 6d. per pound) in 1 pint of methylated spirit. Keep it in a closely stoppered bottle, otherwise the spirit will evaporate quickly.

Glaze may be applied with either rubber, sponge, or brush; in most cases the rubber is most suitable and is most commonly used. It is made in the ordinary way as used for polish, described on pp. 21—25, but it must not be applied with pressure. The glaze is painted on rather than rubbed into the work, which must have been previously bodied in. There seems to be an idea that glaze or something put on bare wood will cause a gloss right off; but nothing will do this. A polish can only be got on wood by varnish, or by bodying in and polish.

When using glaze, the rubber should be made wetter than for polish or spirit; but still there should not be sufficient to drip from it. It should glaze or wet the wood when the rubber is very lightly pressed on it. One or two wipes in the direction of the grain of the wood, with a somewhat quick motion, will put the glaze on. Always let the glaze dry before applying the rubber again to the same place. The coats may be repeated till the gloss is satisfactory, but the film of glaze should never be made a thick one.

If preferred, a sponge may be used exactly as a rubber would be, but it is questionable if there is any advantage gained; it is rather a matter of fancy. When a brush is used, the glaze may be applied as a varnish pure and simple. With a brush a mixture of glaze and French polish, either white or brown, according to the work, in equal quantities, may be used with advantage.

Glaze that is not so satisfactory in appearance as it should be, may sometimes be improved by passing a spirit-rubber lightly over it, though this should be done with great caution, to avoid washing it off. When

carefully and skilfully done, there can be little doubt
that a glazed surface may be often, if not always improved by slightly spiriting it.

To glaze a wide surface, see that it is free from dull
streaks and ridges and oil, and the rubber soft and
free from fluff. Apply the glaze as evenly as possible,
going over the surface several times, until the rubber
is nearly dry; then, with the smallest quantity of oil
and a little spirits, go over the glaze, very lightly
at first, varying the direction of the rubber to avoid
ridges. A *dull*, even surface may be obtained by adding
one-third to one-half of sandarach to the solution of
benzoin, and using the rubber only damp—not saturated.

Old French polished work may often be revived by
being lightly gone over with glaze after the surface has
been washed and cleaned with warm water. This treatment is often considerably better than that commonly
adopted with furniture pastes, polishes, creams, and
revivers of various kinds.

Although the beauty of most furniture woods is
enhanced to the highest degree by French polishing
when well done, there are other processes which, though
not capable of being brought to such perfection, are
much simpler. Among these is wax polishing. This
mode of finishing is remarkably easy, both as regards
materials and manipulation, and the unskilled novice
can manage to wax polish almost as well as an expert.
It is, therefore, a suitable process for the beginner.

Though any wood may be treated by waxing, it is
generally confined to oak, especially after this has been
darkened by fumigation with ammonia—which process
is explained on p. 12. The appearance of oak so
finished is comparatively dull, but it has an attractive-
ness which French polish does not possess for all
eyes.

For antique oak furniture—whether genuine or imitation—wax is the best finish, though varnish is often
used. Wax polish, though it may not give the same
amount of gloss, is clearer and finer. Varnish clogs the

wood, and is apt to give a treacly look to any piece of furniture finished with it.

Mahogany may very appropriately be finished by wax polish, and for many purposes it may be superior to the dulled French polish so often seen. The top of a dining-table is apt to be rendered unsightly from hot plates or dishes injuring the polished surfaces. The heat burns or blisters the hardened shellac of the French polish, and a finish which is not so liable to disfigurement is preferable ; this is found in wax polish. Usually, dining-table tops (unless French polished) are simply oil polished. Waxing is, however, less tedious, and at least as suitable for the purpose, and the readiness with which an accidental marking can be obliterated renders it particularly useful.

Wood stained black, to produce so-called ebony, may be wax polished. The result is certainly a closer approximation to the appearance of real ebony than when the work is French polished in the usual way. By polishing fretwork articles with wax they may easily be made to look better than many of them do when unskilfully French polished.

Though it has been said that any wood may be wax polished, there can be no question that this process answers best on the more coarsely-grained woods, such as oak and ash ; for pine and other light woods of close texture it is not so well suited, unless they have been previously stained.

The ingredients for wax polish are, in the simplest mixture, beeswax and turpentine. Resin and Venice turpentine are occasionally added. Resin is added with the intention of hardening the surface ; but provided the wax be of good quality, these additions are quite unnecessary, if not injurious, and a good result should be got from wax and turps.

Wax and turpentine alone are all the materials necessary to make a good wax polish, and when anything else enters into the composition the mixture is one of a fancy character. It is not proposed to discuss the

D

qualities of beeswax offered for sale, and the polisher
must decide what kind he gets. Some advocate the use
of fine white wax, and possibly a better finish may
sometimes be got with it than with the ordinary yellow
wax, which, however, is the kind generally used;
the only occasions when it might not be so good as the
white are when extreme purity of tone is required
for a light wood. Wood perfectly white is, however,
seldom wax polished.

The way in which wax polish is prepared depends
a good deal on the proportions of the materials. For a
liquid polish, shred the wax finely, and pour the turpentine over it, leaving the two till they are incorporated.
Cold turpentine will dissolve wax slowly, but a more
expeditious method is to melt the wax by heat, and
before it has time to solidify pour the turpentine into it.
Caution is necessary when melting wax, and on no
account should the turpentine be poured into the wax
while it is still on the fire. With ordinary care there is
no danger, and the possibility of a mishap is suggested
merely for the benefit of those who might otherwise
overlook the inflammable character of turpentine vapour.
Should the mixture be either too thick or too thin, there
will be no trouble in altering its consistency afterwards.

To thin a mass which is too stiff, a very moderate
warming, by placing the bottle in hot water, will reduce
it to a more liquid form, as the turpentine already in it
facilitates the change, and more turpentine is added.
To stiffen the mixture, wax should be melted separately,
and the original mixture added to it. The heat of the
freshly-melted wax will probably be sufficient to cause
all the materials to mix. In any case, the wax should
be thoroughly melted before the turpentine is added, as
a lumpy mixture is neither pleasant to work with nor
conducive to good finish. The natural tendency of a
wax polishing mixture, exposed to the air, is to stiffen,
on account of the evaporation of the turpentine. A
considerable time must elapse before there is an appre-
ciable alteration, and the fact that a change does go on,

slowly, is mentioned to remind polishers that if they have a considerable quantity of the mixture standing over, they must not expect it to retain its original consistency unless kept in a closed vessel, such as a tightly corked bottle.

A hint for those who think that the more ingredients a mixture contains the better it must be, and who are not satisfied unless there is a certain amount of resin in their wax polishing paste : always melt the resin first, and add the wax gradually, and constantly stir. Whether resin be used or not, the mixture should be allowed to get quite cold before it is applied to the work.

Although the consistency of wax polish varies considerably, the comparative merits of different degrees of stiffness or fluidity must be considered, so that an intelligent conception of the polisher's aim may be arrived at. Suppose a piece of beeswax, without any admixture of turpentine, is rubbed on a piece of smooth, flat wood. Some of the wax adheres to the surface, which when friction is applied, becomes glossy or polished. The labour, however, is considerable, and though dry wax may do on a flat surface, when mouldings or carvings are to be treated, the difficulties in the way of satisfactory application are considerable. The remedy is to soften the wax so that it may be got into all parts of the work. Melted wax might do, but in putting it on to the wood it becomes cold, and consequently reverts to its original stiffness. We have then to get the wax to a fair working consistency by means of some suitable solvent, which turpentine has proved to be. It is cleanly, inexpensive, and evaporates sufficiently quickly, besides mixing well with the wax. Some polishers prefer what others might think an excess of turpentine. When a stiff paste is used, the wax is apt to be deposited in excessive quantity, necessitating a considerable amount of rubbing, in places to remove it. A fluid polish spreads the wax much more evenly, but no gloss can be obtained till the turpentine has disappeared, either evaporated or been absorbed by the wood.

When the polish has been laid evenly over the work, this does not take long, so a thin mixture may be considered preferable to a very stiff one. A paste of about the consistency of butter in hot weather, might be regarded as a medium. Those who use a wax polish which could be poured would consider this stiff, while others who add very little turpentine, or who believe in resin, would consider it thin. A thick mixture or a thin one may be used, the result depending more on the manipulation of the material than on the material itself; and this manipulation may next be considered.

In the application of wax polish there is almost as great a variety in practice as in proportion of ingredients. The great thing is to have the wax—the turpentine is merely the vehicle for conveying this—evenly and thinly distributed, and so long as this is done it is of small consequence how it is managed. To spread the wax with, some use a piece of rag, while others prefer a stiff brush specially made for the purpose, and both get equally good results. After the wax has been spread the polish is obtained by friction, and the more you rub the brighter the polish will be. The brush or cloth used to rub the wax into the wood should not be employed to give the finishing touches. In this final friction it is essential that the cloth or brush used be perfectly dry, as if it is at all damp no polished surface can be produced. The final polish is best done with a perfectly clean rubber, and three sets of cloths or rubbers may be used. With the first the mixture is to be rubbed on the wood, with the second it is to be rubbed off till a fair amount of polish is got, while with the third the rubbing should be continued till the surface is as bright as it can be got.

The directions which have been given should enable any one to wax-polish wood successfully. Hard dry rubbing, with energetic application is at least as important as the wax and turpentine; for though more simple than the French polishing process, it is more laborious.

CHAPTER VII.

OIL POLISHING AND DRY SHINING.

THE simple process of oil polishing must now receive
attention; and there is still something to admire in a
comparatively dull oiled surface. The process simply
consists of rubbing in linseed oil and polishing with a
soft rag. The oiling and polishing must be continued at
intervals till the requisite shine is obtained. To get the
best results takes time and friction. Oil polishing is
not difficult, but it is decidedly fatiguing and tedious.
The more the surface is rubbed the better, and the
process may be extended over some weeks. Patience
and energetic application are still more essential than
with wax polishing, for to get even the semblance of a
polish or gloss within a week or two with the aid of oil
must not be expected. How long does it take to finish a
thing properly with oil? It may be said the work is
never finished. An oiled surface will always bear more
rubbing than it has had, and will not be deteriorated by
friction; still from one to two months should suffice to
get a good polish which will be durable according to the
amount of labour bestowed upon it during that time.
This is more time than can be devoted to the finishing
touches of a piece of furniture generally nowadays, so it
may almost be considered that oil polishing is an obsolete
process.

Still, it does not follow that because the process is
too long to be remunerative in ordinary work it should
not be worthy of attention, especially as it has merits
which recommend it where speed is not a primary
consideration. One great advantage of it is that it is
much more durable than either French or wax polishes;
it does not blister by heat like the former, nor spoil with
water to such an extent as the latter, with which in general

appearance it may be compared. It is because it does not blister by heat that it is especially useful. An ordinary French polished dining-table top shows the damage caused by hot dishes laid on it, unless great care has been taken. On an oil polished dining-table top the same hot dishes might be placed almost with impunity; and it is chiefly dining-table tops that have prevented oil polishing becoming quite extinct. Though the whole of a table, or anything else, may be polished with oil, it is usual, even when the top is oiled, to polish the legs and frame otherwise.

Linseed oil is the only material used in pure oil polishing, but other ingredients have been used, till it is difficult to recognise the distinction between oil polishing and French polishing. The two processes may overlap to an almost indefinite extent, but with these we have, at present at any rate, nothing to do, and to discuss them might only tend to confuse the novice. Authorities differ on the state in which the linseed oil should be used, some recommending boiled, others raw, and others various proportions of the two. For ordinary work boiled linseed oil is perhaps the better, but this is not intended to imply that those who prefer raw oil are wrong; therefore any oil polisher who has an inclination for some fancy mixture of boiled and raw oils can use it.

The treatment is very much the same as in wax polishing. It consists in rubbing the oil well into the wood, not saturating or flooding, but scrubbing it, and then rubbing long and hard. The process may be repeated almost indefinitely, daily or at longer intervals, till a polish which is deemed sufficient appears. For example, take a table top, rub some oil well into it, and then polish with a rubber formed by wrapping some baize, felt, or similar material round a brick or other suitable block, the purpose of which is, by its weight, to some extent to relieve the polisher from using his muscles in applying pressure. The rubbing should be continued till the surface of the wood is dry. The only perceptible difference in the top will be the darkened appearance caused by the oil, as little or no gloss will appear at first. By repeating the operation, however, a polish will come up gradually, and a surface which in the opinion of many is superior to that of French polish will be the ultimate result. Should the polish sweat, some methylated spirit may be rubbed in. This will dry the surface without spoiling the polish.

Oil polishing is hardly suitable for anything but plain work, on account of the labour required; but any piece of work can be so polished if the necessary time and labour be given to it. Even when it is not deemed practicable to bring up a polish with oil, a very pleasing finish may be given to a piece of work by merely rubbing it with oil. The colour is enriched to an extent which perhaps would hardly be credited by those who have not had frequent opportunities of seeing wood in the white and again after being oiled. In choice mahogany especially the improvement is very marked. Light oak is also greatly improved in tone. Fret-workers who are not proficient in French polishing would be more satisfied with the appearance of anything they make if they simply oiled it instead of coating it with shellac, which has to serve for French polish.

Dry-shining will be found a simple process after the ordinary methods of French polishing have been mastered. Finishing work by dry-shining is the crudest and simplest way in which a gloss can be got on the surface of wood by means of a thin varnish of shellac and methylated spirit. It must not be mistaken for varnish-ing, as this process is ordinarily understood, for it is distinctly a process of French polishing. Even those who have managed to do bodying-up and spiriting-off, or even glazing, will find the operation of dry-shining simple in comparison. It is the nearest approach to varnishing by means of a rubber, instead of a brush, that polishers practise. The wood is varnished with ordinary French polish, applied by means of the polisher's special appliance—the rubber.

Dry-shining, unlike glazing, is not in any degree a substitute for the difficult process of spiriting-off, and those who think to get a high degree of finish on their work by means of dry-shining may give up the illusion. When a really good finish is wanted, French polishing, as it is ordinarily understood, should be chosen, for there is no efficient substitute by which a like result can be got.

Dry-shining can be used in any position where a high degree of finish is not necessary or customary. It is useful for finishing inside work—such as the insides of boxes, drawers, cabinets, and interior parts generally —and is often seen on the fronts of drawers and trays enclosed in a wardrobe. The chief advantages in connection with it are that it can be done expeditiously, and therefore cheaply ; that it sufficiently closes the grain of the wood to prevent dust getting in and clogging it ; and that it gives a certain degree of finish which wood, left in the white or altogether unpolished, does not possess.

The wood is bodied-in without any preparatory filling, but otherwise precisely in the manner directed in Chapter IV. It is not customary to take such precautions to get up a good body as there recommended. A better description of the process is to say that the wood is wiped over with the polish rubber ; not much trouble is usually taken to do more than get the preliminary body worked on. There is no reason why the first body should not be allowed to sink, and the article then be re-bodied if necessary. Much bodying-in would make the work almost as hard as that involved in ordinary French polishing, so that ordinarily the bodying in dry-shining is done more quickly.

When the bodying-in has been done to the satisfaction of the polisher, the rubber is charged with French polish, rather more fully than was recommended for bodying. Instead of being rubbed all over the wood in any direction, it is wiped over in the direction of the grain from end to end of the piece, very much in the manner mentioned in connection with glazing. The rubber may be moved backwards and forwards till dry, but a better way under ordinary circumstances is to let the polish deposited by each rub dry before going over the same place again. When using the rubber in finishing, it should have no oil; and if the former of these two methods is adopted it will be difficult to prevent the polish dragging, so the easier course should be adopted.

CHAPTER VIII.

REPOLISHING AND REVIVING.

HAVING once mastered the fundamental principle of polishing, as explained in Chap. III., it is a comparatively easy task to give to a plain piece of wood a level and lustrous surface ; and by the use of stains that can be bought ready prepared, a fair imitation of any given wood can be obtained with but little labour. But the polisher who wishes to hold his own against all comers, must be able to do more than merely to stain and polish a plain piece of new wood.

When dealing with old work that requires repolishing, all dirt, grease, and furniture paste must be removed by careful washing with soda and warm water and powdered pumice-stone or bath brick. It can then be French polished, or a fresher and more satisfactory appearance may be given by applying one or two coats of brown hard spirit varnish—such as can be bought at an oil and colour merchant's—carefully with a camel-hair brush.

When varnished work has to be dealt with, first clean off all the varnish and then repolish in the way described in previous chapters, except that filling will probably be dispensed with. The varnish can generally be more easily removed by scraping than by papering. With care the varnish can be washed off with soda or potash and water, but on account of the liability to injure the wood it is scarcely advisable to adopt this method.

For removing polish from flat surfaces, the steel scrapers as used by cabinet-makers are the best tools to use. In turned and other work which has an uneven surface the old coating can nearly all be got off by the application of strong hot soda water, to which may be added some oxalic acid in difficult cases. When a large quantity of work has to be treated, use the following mixture :—½ lb. American potash, ½ lb. soft soap, ½ lb. rock ammonia, 1 lb. washing soda, 3 ounces of nitric acid, 1 gallon of water. Apply with a fibre or scrubbing brush, taking care of the hands. Swill off with plenty of clean water. When the work is dry, oil and fill in ; then repolish.

Spirit varnish can be removed by washing with methylated spirit, which redissolves the lac. This is both a tedious and somewhat expensive method, which need be resorted to only for delicate mouldings and other work which cannot well be cleaned by scraping or by scouring with some liquid which, though it would remove the varnish, might stain and so spoil the wood. Methylated spirit being neutral may be used on any wood, as it will not affect the colour.

When dealing with cabinets or other built-up work, the process of repolishing will be simplified somewhat by taking apart as much as convenient. It is a good plan to unhinge all doors, to remove all carvings that may be screwed on from the back, and to remove all knobs, brass-fittings, etc.—not forgetting to put some tallying mark on each piece which might be liable to misplacement. Thus the doors can be better handled on the bench, the corners of panels can be worked up better, and the carvings can be varnished better. When the carvings are planted on, as is often done, a much cleaner job is made if these are first removed ; for it is a difficult task to polish the open carvings equal to the flat surface.

Sometimes polished work is disfigured by fine little lines which are caused by cracks, resulting from sweating. These lines become visible through the dust settling on the exuding oil. This disfigurement can be averted almost entirely by occasionally carefully wiping with a soft damp cloth. Sweating is not entirely preventible, but when the oil has ceased to exude, which may not be for some months, the work may be repolished with advantage.

The perfectly level,' brilliant polish found on new German pianos fills many an English French-polisher with envy. Unfortunately, this brilliant polish does not last long, and the majority of the pianos soon have a greasy, cracked appearance. Indeed, there are but few of these pianos with a polish gained by the legitimate process of French-polishing. This brilliant, level polish is gained by a very liberal use of gum sandarach, and when the polishing is completed the pianos are set aside in a clean, hot room, 'which has the effect of causing the polish or gums to flow to one dead level. Some makers use varnish very freely, and, before passing to the hot room, level this by means of pumice powder, tripoli, putty powder, and sometimes flour.

When the requisite number of coats of varnish have been laid, the surface is levelled with fine glass-paper and linseed-oil, or by the slower process of felt rubber and pumice powder. After being wiped perfectly clean, a rubber made'of soft flannel, or, better still, of old silk, is used to rub carefully and lightly in a circular direction with tripoli powder and oil, till the surface is perfectly level and inclined to be bright; it is then rubbed with dry putty powder and silk, and finally brightened with flour.

The surface should be left perfectly free from any trace of the polishing powders; neglect of this accounts for the white patches sometimes seen on the German pianos. These patches are not so deep as they appear at first sight, and may often be removed with flour emery and linseed oil or turps without disturbing the polish.

To renovate the polish on these pianos is difficult, but when it is not very bad, a reviver made of equal parts linseed oil, lime water, and turps is generally effective. The lime water and oil are first thoroughly mixed; then the turps are added, and the mixture is applied by means of wadding. The surface is wiped off

with a rag, and finished with a clean, soft rag-swab, made
fairly moist with methylated spirit. Should any trace
of grease still remain, change to a clean place of the
already moist rag, and sprinkle a few spots of glaze on
its face, or, better still, wipe the face of the glaze rubber
over the face of the clean swab.

Should this method prove ineffective it will be
necessary to repolish, first removing the sweat or rough-
ness by fine glass-paper and oil, or by washing with
weak soda-water and pumice powder. The polish used
should be made with spirit instead of naphtha, and, to
ensure its lasting qualities, it should be bodied up one
day and finished the next.

To darken the birch frame of a chair, wipe it over
with asphaltum dissolved in turpentine (one pennyworth in half a pint of turps). This stains without
giving a painted appearance; should there be any
difficulty in obtaining asphaltum, vandyke brown may
be used, mixed to a thin paste with liquid ammonia—or
with a strong solution of common washing-soda. This
is thinned with water, till of the required tone, which
will readily be found by trying its effect on any odd piece
of wood. If French polish cannot be applied, the most
suitable thing to use is brown hard spirit varnish.

For restoring polish that has faded from damp
or exposure to the sun, those stains which are used
to stain the common woods will not be suitable.
It may be convenient to remove only the upper surface of the polish, to colour the faded portion so as to
match its surroundings, and to repolish the whole.
When the polish is not very bad, it is generally
sufficient to smooth it well with a piece of worn
glass-paper. When it is much scratched or faded,
methylated spirit should be sprinkled upon it, and the
surface well rubbed with No. 1 glass-paper, applied with
a circular motion; it will then be found that only the
upper surface of the polish will be removed. Before
repolishing, it is advisable first to wash the article with
water to which a little common washing soda has been

added. This will remove any dirt, furniture paste, etc. ; a little pumice powder or powdered bath brick may be used to assist.

After the necessary cleaning-off of dirt, etc., has been accomplished, any bruises must be removed, either by scraping out or by bringing up level, by means of a hot iron and moisture, or by filling up with hard stopping, or by the still better method given on page 69. When this has been done, and all defective parts made good, the surface must be wiped over with an oily rag ; it assists the new polish to take kindly to the old. In scraping out the bruises, in cleaning-off level any new piece, and in cleaning-off the polish, it is probable that light patches may be made. More especially will these be made apparent if the damaged portion has been previously coloured up by stains, dry colours, or dyed polish.

For colouring-up or matching, it is generally sufficient, if the wood in hand is mahogany, to wipe over the damaged portion with red oil, which consists of ¼ lb. of alkanet root steeped in 1 pint of linseed-oil, working up with red polish. Should the wood be walnut, many a little blemish and scratch in soft resinous varnish may be matched by wiping over with a solution of one pennyworth of asphaltum dissolved in ½ pint turps. Should the defect be a piece of sap or other light portion, go over the light portion several times with the polish rubber to prevent the grain from rising, and then saturate a small tuft of wadding with 3 parts of methylated spirits to 1 part of polish ; on this wadding place a small quantity of vandyke brown or brown umber, mix well, and carefully wipe over the light portions, thinning out with spirits if too dark, picking up a little more colour if not dark enough, adding a little black if required.

Matching stains are used in French polishing because light and dark places often occur in the best selected woods, and in stained work, owing to the difference in the direction of the grain. To tone or harmonise the entire surface to one uniform shade, is technically called matching or colouring up, and requires a little tact and a good eye for colour. On large flat surfaces coloured polish may be used with advantage, but for small work it would be better to take a small tuft of wadding and wet it with 1 part polish to 3 parts spirits. With this take up a little yellow ochre and just a trace of umber or vandyke brown. Press the wadding well on the back of a piece of worn-out glass-paper to equalise, and mix well. Try the effect on an odd corner of the work; if too dark thin out with spirits; if not dark enough pick up more colour, or wipe over twice. Having gained the right shade, apply lightly with a straight or wavy motion as required. This would enable one to match the oak, but any wood can be matched by using suitable pigments, a red tinge being usually given by the addition of a few drops of Bismarck brown stain. Though it is possible to proceed to polish direct, yet it would be safer to set the stain by giving a coat of thin spirit varnish, and allow this to get quite dry before polishing. In matching-up satin walnut, the polisher must use judgment, for the work can hardly be regarded as mechanical. The stain must depend on the colour or tint of the lighter parts, and of the darker parts to which they are to be matched. Generally a little weak brown stain will do what is required. When necessary, it can be altered slightly in colour by the addition of other pigments, according to the tints desired.

In matching, the wavy appearance of some woods may be given by a tremulous movement of the hand, and the mottled appearance of others by dabbing with a badger softener or clean, soft dusting-brush while the colour is still wet. Veins either black or red may be given by picking up a little dry black or red stain on the corner of the tuft of wadding and applying it carefully, taking some adjacent portion as a guide for pattern. For rosewood, red stain and dry black may be used in combination; for birch or oak, use yellow ochre

When the work in hand is large, and requires staining all over, and it is not possible to gain the desired result by means of dyed polish applied with the rubber, the colours should be mixed in a pot with 3 parts of spirit to one of polish, and applied with a camel-hair brush. The work is not so liable to get patchy with two or more coats of weak stain as with one strong one.

After laying on the stain allow a few minutes to elapse for it to set, then smooth down with a piece of worn, fine glass-paper, and give a coat of thin brush polish or spirit varnish. This will set the colours previous to polishing, which can be proceeded with in · about ten minutes. Mahogany, rosewood, and walnut, if not inlaid, are generally improved by the use of a polish tinged by the addition of a little red stain. Other colours may also be mixed with polish to be applied with the rubber. When using these dyed polishes cease when just the right tinge is attained ; another rubber may be used to finish off with clear polish.

In repolishing work the foundation having been already laid, the polish is not required quite so thick as in polishing the bare wood. In the final stage, when finishing-off, any trace of greasiness may be effectually removed by well-rubbing with a swab of clean, soft rag, fairly damp (not wet) with spirits, on the face of which has been sprinkled a few drops of glaze.

Colours in a dry state known as pigments, such as venetian red, yellow ochre, vegetable black or lampblack, umbers, vandyke brown, chromes, orange and lemon, greens, blues, flake white, etc., are useful. By the aid of these, the polisher is enabled to match woods and restore faded polish, far more expeditiously than can be done by staining or using dyed polish or varnish. Work that might puzzle the inexperienced for hours can be done in a few minutes by a knowledge of the use of dry colours. They are used in some stains by mixing with ammonia, glue size, pearlash, soda, and they are used to colour the "filling-in" of whiting and turps to make it match the various woods. Venetian red is used for mahogany, umber for walnut, black for ebony, and sometimes to give an appearance of age to oak by making the grain appear dirty.

Sometimes the polisher has a job passed to him that, properly speaking, ought to be done by the painter. The quick drying nature of the solutions of shellac, with which the polisher is the better acquainted, obtains for him the preference. For example shields, etc., for decorative purposes that may require five different colours and a coat of varnish, can be coloured ready for fixing within twenty-four hours. To do this lime blue, chrome yellow, vegetable black, flake white, and vermilionette or any other colours should be mixed with ordinary French polish to the consistency of thin paint, thinning out when necessary with methylated spirits. Three coats of colour can be laid on, stencil patterns cut and painted, borders and edges lined, and the whole finished with a coat of white hard varnish within twelve hours. To prevent the white getting a yellowish tinge, it is well to mix it with transparent polish made from white shellac.

To make imitation marble which wears well, give several coats of flake white mixed in polish ; then put in the veins of blue or black with feathers, afterwards giving a coat of white thinned out with spirits. This has the effect of making the veining appear beneath the surface. When dry it is finished by giving a coat of good quality copal varnish.

E

CHAPTER IX.

HARD STOPPING OR BEAUMONTAGE.

THE French polisher who does much repairing and repolishing, finds hard stopping, or beaumontage, exceedingly useful, for if carefully selected as regards colour, it is difficult to distinguish it from the wood when polished over.

The polisher may be called upon to repolish furniture from which little bits of veneer are chipped off, or in which some bruise, crack or blister, presents itself. With his glue-pot, veneer, and cauls at hand, the cabinet-maker might let in little bits of wood, or run in hot glue, and apply cauls, hand-screws or weights, as may be required. The polisher may be out of reach of such appliances, and to call in assistance would take away all his profit, besides hindering him with his job. Something that will enable him to make level all defects in a short time and to proceed at once with his polishing is found in hard stopping.

The skilled cabinet-maker should make all his joints fit closely, and arrange his nails and screws in such a position that their heads will be out of sight, and leave no holes or defects to need filling up. But he will find it difficult to select all his wood and to prevent any slip or accident so that his work shall have neither flaw, shaken, or hole, and he will welcome a composition that will fill up and obliterate all defects. A mixture of beeswax and resin in about equal parts is used by some for such a purpose, and it is usually made up in two colours—red for mahogany and brown for walnut.

The cabinet-maker has little need for such a composition as beaumontage when making new work, but it is a boon to those who have to depend largely upon repairs and chance jobs for their livelihood, and to those who have made some useful or ornamental article with a packing case or other cheap class of wood. With such material it will be found extremely difficult so to select the wood and cut it that a nail or screw-hole, or a flaw, does not occasionally present itself.

Beaumontage has advantages over putty or beeswax and resin. Putty, in drying, always shrinks, showing plainly an indentation in the case of cracks and screw-holes. If used on white wood before staining and polishing, its oily nature prevents the stains sinking into the wood as deeply as in the parts untouched by it, thus causing the work to have a patchy appearance. In beeswax and resin, the chief fault is the want of variety, the colours being limited. In most cases it is kept in an iron ladle or large spoon, which is not convenient for a polisher to carry with him in his kit when going away from home to work.

Hard stopping can be made up in an infinite variety of colours like sticks of sealing-wax, and it can, with care, be selected to match any wood. It will not shrink, but retains a level surface and takes the polish well. These points alone are sufficient to establish its superiority over beeswax and resin or putty. The greater the variety of colours the more its usefulness becomes apparent. It gives a better chance of matching, and often saves the staining which might be necessary if little bits of veneer were let in.

Beaumontage is easily made, but can be bought ready for use at most places where veneers and fancy woods are sold for about one penny per stick; it is generally called "stopping-out wax." It is also sold at 1s. 6d. per lb. in various colours.

To make a hard stopping, plane up two pieces of wood about ⅜ in. thick, 15 or 18 in. long, and 9 in. wide, one of which should be screwed on the bench. Take a cupful of any common shellac, put it in a tin or iron pot (a half-pound mustard or coffee tin will do), add a tea-spoonful of powdered resin, a piece of beeswax the

size of half a walnut, and a teaspoonful of powdered lemon chrome. Heat till the whole is
melted, stir with a stick to properly mix, and pour a
little of the melted composition on the fixed board.
Then gather it up by means of a scraper or knife,
roll out between the hands, and while still plastic roll
into sticks between the two boards by passing the
uppermost or loose board to and fro. If the loose board
is made warm by keeping it before the fire when not in
use, it gives a better result. Care must be taken not to
get the composition *too hot*, as it spoils by boiling. It
will require practice before perfectly round sticks can be
made.

Proceed to make sticks of stopping in the following
way : Pour sufficient of this mixture to make two sticks
of this colour ; then add a little yellow ochre, and
make two more ; these will give two shades that will do
nicely for oak. Add a little brown umber, warm up
again, and roll out two more ; these will do for light
walnut. Add a little more umber and make sticks for
dark walnut ; add Venetian red for mahogany, and a
little black for rosewood, and finally finish up with black
for ebony. By varying the amount of dry colours any
number of shades can be obtained, and it will be found
convenient to make the colours in the order suggested.
If the darker shades are made first it will be found
difficult to obtain the lighter ones, owing to the dark
colours clinging to the sides of the pot.

To use this hard stopping, a piece of flat metal that
will retain heat for a few minutes will be wanted. A
worn-out 6-in. flat file in a handle would do admirably.
For an inch or so from the point the file teeth should
be removed by the aid of a grindstone. To stop a
crack, nail or screw-hole, select a stick of stopping the
required shade, bearing in mind that if the wood you
are at work upon is intended to be afterwards stained,
it will be necessary to select stopping of the colour which
the article is intended to be when finished ; for the
stopping itself cannot be stained after it is in the wood.

Have the iron hot, and hold it in the right hand ; with the other press the stick of stopping against it, as the stopping is run into the defective part, somewhat similarly to the way in which the tinker uses his copper bit and solder. When the crack is well filled and a little over, press the stopping well in while the iron is still warm. When cold, clean off level with a sharp chisel, scraper, or knife, and then use glass-paper.

It will help the stopping to hold in a shallow bruise if a few holes are made in the bruised part with a brad-awl or chisel. In burr walnut, or other fancy figured wood, round holes are best ; in straight-grained wood, such as bay or mahogany, a straight cut from a chisel or knife is preferable.

A bruise may often be raised level with the surface again. Where this can be done it is preferable to the use of beaumontage. It is done by pouring methy-lated spirit in the hollow which forms the bruise and setting it on fire, blowing it out before the spirit is ex-hausted to prevent it burning the wood. It will be found in most cases that the bruise has come up level with the surface ; but if badly bruised, it will require more than one application of spirit, the flame of which must always be blown out before the spirit itself is entirely burnt away. Bruises of nearly every description can be raised in this way. A hot iron applied near to the dent which has been wetted will also bring it up level.

If veneered work is blistered, make a number of round holes, or straight slits in the raised part and run some stopping in, and press down with the hot iron. With care this is a more expeditious plan than opening the blister, putting hot glue under, and applying weights or pressure. The stopping holds the veneer down like pegs or nails.

Beeswax, made up of various colours, will be found useful. Slight fissures in the veneers, imperfect joints, or places where the stopping has not quite filled up, may be made much more presentable by the aid of this. Heel-ball and cobbler's wax, though sometimes used,

cannot be recommended, as they seldom take polish
well. Coloured beeswax, made up in the form and size
of heel-balls, will be found convenient, and it can be
made, as described for stopping, by melting the wax and
adding the various colours, then running it into moulds.
A few 1¼ in. holes bored through a piece of hard wood,
about ½ in. thick, and this screwed to another piece,
makes a convenient mould into which to run the melted
wax. When cold, the discs of wax are easily removed
if the two pieces of wood be unscrewed.

In making good the defects in work that is old, and
which has been previously polished, it will be found
that the necessary cleaning off will leave a bare patch ;
this should be wiped over with a little linseed oil, then
bodied-up, and a few hours or a night allowed in which
to harden before finally bodying-up and finishing.

CHAPTER X.

TREATMENT OF FLOORS.

THE custom of staining and varnishing floors has, apart
from sanitary and hygienic reasons, and its lightening
of the daily labour of cleaning, much to recommend
it. The margin of the floors, from 12 in. to 36 in.
wide, is stained and either varnished or polished, and
art, oriental, or other squares and rugs are used in the
middle only, instead of the whole of the floor being
covered with carpet ; the margin left on the stairs by the
stair carpet is similarly treated. From an artistic stand-
point much might be said in favour of this plan. The
working man generally contents himself with simply
staining and varnishing in some neutral colour—mostly
in imitation of walnut. His wealthier neighbour has a
margin of parquetry, made of various kinds of wood in
veneer or blocks, carefully selected and joined together
by experienced hands in geometrical designs. These are
generally finished by the process known as wax polish.
Whether in the near future these artistic borderings will
be used in the homes of the artisan remains to be seen.
At present he has to content himself with floorcloth,
linoleum, or stained floorboards.

In America they have what are called " hard-wood
floors," made of veneers cut to various designs and
secured in position by strong cloth or canvas backing,
and made up in designs, usually 1 ft. 6 in. by 4 ft.
for covering the central part of a floor. For the
margins a separate design is worked out, usually in
12 ft. lengths and of various widths. The boarded
floor having been made perfectly level, this parquetry is secured to it by fine brads driven through
nearly every piece of wood ; these brads are punched a

little below the surface, and the holes filled up with putty coloured to match the wood. After cleaning off and glass-papering the hard wood, it is finished by oil or wax polish.

It may not be amiss here to offer a few suggestions to those who are not quite able to decide whether their carpets shall fit close to the walls, or whether a square carpet shall be laid in the centre, leaving a margin all round to be stained, or, as is often the case, covered with some kind of floorcloth.

The disadvantage of a close-fitted carpet is that it cannot, without difficulty, be taken up, and as this is not done frequently, dirt accumulates. A square of carpet, however it is laid, can be taken up and re-laid without much trouble. On the score of economy, strong arguments can be given in favour of squares. The initial cost is considerably less, for there is little or no cutting to waste, even when the square is made up of ordinary carpeting; whereas, in a room having a carpet closely fitted to the floor, a considerable quantity may be, and often is, cut to waste. Thus saving is effected by using a smaller carpet, there being no waste in material. The only objection to squares that can be seriously urged has merely to do with the question of appearance, as some people think that a floor which is carpeted all over looks more comfortable.

Preparing the Floor. — Before anything in the way of staining can be done the floor must be made perfectly level. If it is an old flooring, pull up any nails which have been used for fastening carpets. The nail-holes may be filled with putty, but in recesses and dark corners it may not be necessary to take this trouble. All floor nails should be punched in at least one-eighth of an inch below the surface. If the boards do not fit closely together, fill in all openings with strips of wood planed wedge shape. These should be brushed over with glue on both sides, then driven well home with a mallet, and allowed to stand till next day before planing off level. If an ordinary smoothing plane is used for this purpose it will be found impossible to plane lengthways close up to the skirting board. A useful plane for such a purpose is known as a bull-nose, a section of which is shown in Fig. 8. With this it is possible to smooth the floor to within a quarter of an inch of the skirting; the remaining portion can be smoothed with a chisel and finished with glass-paper. The floor, whether newly laid or not, must be perfectly free from grease and paint. To ensure this it is a wise plan to give it a good scouring

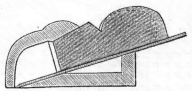

Fig. 8.—Bull-nose Plane in Section.

with hot water, in which common soda has been dissolved instead of soap. When the floor is perfectly dry give another rub down with No. 1 glass-paper. The best thing to use to scrub a dirty floor is a common brick, or a Bath brick. The brick is dipped in soda water and used like a scrubbing brush. Lump pumice stone is also used for this purpose.

For the purpose of stopping up nail-holes, etc., plaster of Paris is sometimes recommended. Should it be used, it must be done *previous* to any staining. Putty is the material in most general use, but on no account must it be used with stains that are mixed with water. As putty is a mixture of whiting and linseed oil, this will prevent the stain sinking into the wood; consequently a patchy appearance will be the result. Should the stains have a spirit, oil, or varnish basis, it is of little moment when the holes are filled up, though it is wise to give the floor at least one coat of stain first.

The putty or plaster should be coloured to match the stain by the addition of some colouring medium.

If the floor be a dirty or discoloured one, it is advisable to plane all over the portion to be stained, otherwise the difference between new and old, clean and dirty surfaces will probably be plainly discernible.

So far we have presumed that the floor is of common spruce or deal. Should it be of oak, equal pains must be taken in its preparation.

A simple and effective way to stain floors is to take one pint of methylated spirit; in this dissolve four ounces of shellac; then add, for a walnut colour, as much brown umber as will give the tone required in two or more applications. Similarly, Venetian red may be added for mahogany, and yellow ochre for pine. Apply this with a brush to the boards, and when dry, smooth down with fine glass-paper. By wiping over with a little linseed oil on flannel it will be kept fresh looking; or it may be finished bright by giving two coats of best oak varnish. It also forms a capital basis for wax or French polish.

Marking Out the Floor.—For good workmanship it is essential that the floor should be marked out, and all staining done to a clean cut edge, particularly if it is intended to finish with a border or stencil pattern. In deciding what width the margin shall be, allow at least 3 in. of the stained portion to be underneath the carpet; thus, on laying down the carpet, if the edge is found to stand 18 in. from the skirting, mark the margin to be stained at least 21 in. wide. This marking out is sometimes dispensed with, the work being done in a haphazard fashion, and sometimes the carpet is fixed previous to staining and varnishing. Both methods are to be deprecated; they stamp the work as having been done by inexperienced hands.

Staining.—Unquestionably the best method is that of using stains first, then sizing and varnishing, unless it should be thought that varnish is *too* bright and glaring. In that case it may be finished by wax polish, oil polish, or French polishing; but it must be borne in mind that for the last-named process the floor must be exceptionally well cleaned up.

Varnish is to be recommended generally for use in ordinary rooms. It requires less attention to keep in order than wax. An occasional coat of varnish will restore the margin to its original gloss. Wax-polished floors require rubbing frequently, and they cannot be washed without destroying the gloss, so the style of finish is not strongly advocated, except for floors used for dancing purposes. As traffic over waxed floors soon destroys their gloss, it is advisable to have plenty of mats or rugs lying about, especially near the doorway.

Oiling has few, if any, advantages beyond the cheapness of the work, and can hardly be recommended as suitable for ordinary dwelling-houses. At its best, an oiled floor never looks as well as one that is varnished, and it is only where there is much traffic, and when expense is a prime consideration, that this is the most suitable finish.

Floors are not often French polished, but spirit varnish of good quality may be used on floors that are not subject to much hard wear.

Whatever may be the method decided upon for the finish, staining must first be done. This is usually in imitation of oak or walnut; but there is no particular reason—beyond custom—why other colours should not be used.

Several well-known makes of stain are in the market which can be confidently recommended for the purpose. Those who desire to make their own stain will find full particulars in Chapter XI.; but there is no better recipe than vandyke brown, ammonia, and water. The proportions are of little importance. The vandyke brown is mixed with the ammonia to form a thin paste; water must afterwards be added to reduce the strength and liquefy the stain. A thin paste is mentioned, and it must be understood that a thick paste is not satisfactory; but the mixture may be diluted to almost any

extent without detriment. Care must be taken that the
brown is thoroughly mixed. The mixed brown and
ammonia paste may be kept as a stock preparation to be
used with water as may be required, or it may have
water added and be kept in a diluted state ready for
use. It is advisable to mix at least as much as will
suffice to do a room entirely, and so avoid a difficulty in
matching a fresh mixture to an exact shade. As to the
quantity required, it has already been pointed out (*see
p.* 16) that one gallon will cover one hundred square yards,
one gallon of varnish being required for the same surface.

When the stain is all ready in a paint kettle or other
convenient receptacle, select a large sash tool, as used by
painters, and a fitch, or small sash tool, for doing
the edges. Apply the stain plentifully, lengthways of
the floor boards, commencing at the right or left of the
fireplace and working round to the door. Recommence
on the other side of the fireplace, working round towards the door again, so allowing free ingress to the
room without interfering with the staining operations.
Allow the stain several hours to dry. Should the colour
not be sufficiently dense repeat the operation as before,
bearing in mind that two coats of a lighter shade will
give a better result and be more evenly distributed than
one coat of darker colour. It is strongly advised that
experiments should be made on odd pieces of wood to
get the desired colour before commencing the floor.

Care should be taken, especially if potash or soda
has been used in it, not to let the stain get on a
painted skirting-board.

If a simple margin of one uniform colour is all that
is wanted, it will now be ready for one or two coats of
clear size. Size is used to economise varnish ; it is much
cheaper and fills the grain of the wood, which thus
absorbs less varnish, and allows it to remain on the
surface where it is wanted. If the varnish sinks there
is comparatively little gloss. The size may be obtained
of almost any oil and colourman. It is applied to the
floor like the stain, and must be allowed to become

thoroughly dry before varnishing. After sizing, fill up with plaster of Paris, made into a thin paste with water, all nail-holes and crevices in which it has been found impracticable to insert slips of wood.

Combined Stains and Varnish.—With a view to simplifying the process, varnish makers have put upon the market combined stains and varnish. These stains claim to give tones varying from light oak to dark walnut ; the latter colour is gained by giving successive coats. Their use is not strongly recommended, except where the lighter tones have been chosen, and then the work is given a finishing coat of good oak varnish to equalise it in appearance and body.

For a wax-polished floor it is only necessary to stain, and then when dry, wax-polish in accordance with the instructions given in the chapter devoted to that subject.

The same remarks apply to oil finishing, except that it will be understood that the same care is not necessary as with furniture. Indeed, on a floor it is useless to get polish with oil, which is useful to enrich the colour of the stain, and that is all.

A very useful stain may be made by thinning ordinary paint with turpentine. Of course the turpentine causes the paint to dry flat or dead, but a coat of varnish will soon alter this.

Decorative Borders.—Some rooms may be improved in appearance by a decorative border, as shown in the suggestive illustrations (Fig. 9). These borders need not be elaborate in design ; simple yet bold patterns give the better general effect—on the same principle that the carpet designer does not rely so much on the elaboration of detail as on the careful selection and blending of colours.

Presuming that the floor margin has been stained brown and the inner edge left cut clean, mark out the portion it is intended to decorate. The groundwork of this may be pine, satinwood, or light mahogany. The colours selected for the stencil should then be in marked contrast, such as rosewood, black or brown. Stencil-plates may be bought, or they may be cut out of paper-hanger's lining paper, care being taken to cut them

Fig. 9.—Suggestions for Border Ornaments for Floor.

clean and sharp, and to leave in sufficient tie-pieces or break lines to hold the stencil intact. Give the paper stencil-plates a coat of linseed oil to strengthen and preserve them.

Mix the stencil paint to the colour decided upon and the consistency of stiff paste; take up a little of this with a stencil-brush, Fig. 10, which is specially made for the purpose, and spread it on a slate or smooth piece of board, then stipple it through the stencil-plate. If care is taken to keep the stencil-plate motionless on the work during the process of applying the paint, and the brush has not been charged with too much at a time, the pattern should be clearly and sharply imprinted on the floor.

Should the imitation of tiles be attempted, mark them out to correspond with the boards—that is, with boards 7 in. wide set out the tiles 7 in. square—and these

Fig. 10.—Stencil Brush.

may be subdivided at pleasure. The reason for this precaution should be apparent; should the boards shrink, it certainly would not look well to see a row of tiles apparently cracked.

Black or other dark colour lines of at least $\frac{1}{2}$ in. wide should divide the plain from the decorated portions of a floor, and on the inner edge of the decoration a width of at least 3 in. should be stained the same colour as the margin. The lines may be put in with a lining fitch or pencil, using the thick paint as advised for the stencils; or suitable colours may be mixed with equal parts of French polish and spirits. Imitation tiles should be outlined with black or brown lines at least $\frac{1}{16}$ in. wide. A glance at some printed floorcloth or linoleum will show how this is done.

Finishing Processes.—All staining and decorating being finished, the work is then sized, care being taken to use the size only moderately hot, and to work the brush about as little as possible to avoid breaking up the colours; it is then allowed to get quite dry. It is next smoothed down with fine worn glass-paper; all dust is removed, and one or two coats of good varnish, such as hard oak, are laid on with a brush, starting next to the fireplace, as advised in staining. Whatever varnish is used, it should be laid on with a brush, and it may be noted, as in staining, that two coats thinly laid on are better than one applied thickly. In many cases one coat is all that is needed. Let the varnish stand several days to harden before allowing it to be walked on.

The feet of chairs, or other portions of furniture resting upon the varnished surface, should be kept from scratching it by gluing on to them pieces of cloth or wash-leather. Should the varnish get scratched or show white marks, try the effect of wiping over with a little linseed oil.

CHAPTER XI.

STAINS.

Some general information on processes of staining wood is given in Chapter II. The present chapter will deal chiefly with the making of various kinds of stains.

The following recipes apply to the staining of common woods to imitate the more costly :—

Walnut.—(a) 1 pennyworth nut-galls, 1 pennyworth Vandyke brown, ¼ lb. American potash, 1 gal. water. Cost, fourpence per gallon. The nut-galls should be crushed and mixed with the potash, and the water added hot. The stain may be used hot or cold. A little brown umber may be included in the mixture if desired. (b) Mix Vandyke brown, or equal parts Vandyke brown and brown umber, into a thin paste with liquor ammonia ; thin down to the required tone with water. It is not absolutely necessary to use ammonia in the walnut stain, but it is better to do so. The smell will soon evaporate, and it can hardly be objectionable if the stain stands for a few days before using it. Caustic soda or potash may be used instead of ammonia, but against these objections may be urged. (c) ¼ lb. asphaltum dissolved in 1 pt. turpentine or coal-tar naphtha. This is useful for common work, but requires to be coated with brush polish or varnish before it will polish readily. (d) 1 gal. strong vinegar, 1 lb. burnt umber, ½ lb. rose pink, ½ lb. Vandyke brown. Apply with brush or sponge. (e) 2 oz. of common black privet berries, such as grow in most gardens, may be gathered in the winter season ; ½ pt. solution of ammonia. Applied to pine woods to be polished or varnished, this is said to give a very good imitation, hard to detect from real walnut. (f) For cheap work,

F

such as floor-margins, use ordinary glue-size, coloured
by the addition of brown umber and a very little black
or red. This should be applied with a brush, and then
well rubbed in with a piece of rag. One or more coats
may be given, according to the tone required. When
dry, smooth down with fine glass-paper before applying
the varnish. (*g*) When the staining of floors first came
into vogue, the stain largely adopted was a solution
of 1 oz. permanganate of potash to a quart of water.
Though purple, this dries a rich brown colour when
laid, and has the merit of imitating no particular wood,
but gives a colour that harmonises with most carpets.
(For further information on staining floors see Chapter X.)
(*h*) 2 ozs. Vandyke brown, 2 ozs. American potash, 1 oz.
bichromate of potash, a piece of soda the size of a walnut,
the same amount of sulphate of copper, a small piece of
sulphate of iron, 2 ozs. nitric acid, and 1 gallon of water.
Boil the water, brown, bichromate, soda, and sulphates
until melted and well mixed. Then add the American
potash, which must be first put in a little water, otherwise it will effervesce over the sides of the pot. When
lukewarm add the acid. (*i*) Extract of walnut is now
looked upon as an old-time method, owing partly to the
difficulty of obtaining the green walnuts when out of
season. Something always at hand is preferred. The
extract can easily be made by bruising the walnuts
and adding common washing soda and hot water.
(*j*) Ordinary white wood can be given the appearance
of black walnut by first thoroughly drying the wood,
and when warmed, coating it two or three times with
a strong solution of walnut peel. The wood thus
treated is washed over when nearly dry with a solution of bichromate of potash, one part in five parts of
boiling water. When thoroughly dried, rub and polish.

Oak.—(*a*) Wipe over with crushed asphaltum dissolved in turpentine (¼ lb. to the pint). (*b*) Take some
brown umber, mix into a thin paste with liquor ammonia, then thin out with water till the required shade
is gained. (*c*) One of the simplest methods of staining

deal and obtaining the dull polish seen on very dark oak is to stain it and then varnish with flatting varnish as follows :—First see that the work is entirely free from glue, grease, and rough places, and then stain twice with dark oak stain, softening down between each coat, before the stain dries, with a soft brush, called a badger, which will take out brush marks left in staining. This must be done thoroughly and quickly, as any touching up is almost sure to show. When the stain is dry, rub it down with a piece of canvas, not glass-paper, which is very liable to leave white marks. The canvas can be got more easily into the hollows of columns and mouldings. In all stained work, the less glass-paper used, even in preparing the work, the better. In no case may the paper be used across the grain, as it is sure to show. Coat twice with best clear size, rubbing down between each coat as explained for staining. If the work is varnished with good flatting varnish, and then hard rubbed with a soft rag or piece of silk, the surface should have a nice dull gloss. (d) The following mixture allows of great latitude in shade as well as in actual colour, according to the quantity of water :—Vandyke brown mixed with liquor ammonia, and then diluted with water, a little Bismarck brown being added to give the reddish tint required. (e) Another good stain may be made by dissolving bichromate of potash in water. By modifying this with Vandyke brown or Stephens' walnut stain, almost any required shade of brown may be obtained. Alone it gives rather too much of an orange hue, so some persons prefer to add a little walnut-stain, which removes the reddish cast or harshness. It is easy to give several applications if one is not strong enough. Apply the stain with a brush, and allow it to turn colour by action of light and air. This stain is useful for a variety of purposes, thus: Light oak may be made to match brown or pollard oak ; common bay-wood to match superior mahogany ; and common mahogany to represent old Spanish. No hard-and-fast rule can be laid down as to whether the work should be

previously oiled or not. Some claim that if it is not
oiled the stain will strike deeper; on the other hand,
experience proves that if the work is oiled first the stain
is more evenly distributed, and that the grain does not
rise to the same extent; but it should be well rubbed
in, not left merely on the top of the oil. Permanganate
of potash may be used instead of bichromate of potash
(*see* Stains for Walnut, p. 81). (*f*) Yellow pine can
be stained to resemble oak in colour by very simple
means, but if it is intended that the figure should also
be imitated, this will be found a more difficult task. A
rich dark colour can be gained by dissolving 2 lbs. of
patent size in 1 pt. of water, adding some brown umber to
give a brown shade, applying while still hot with a
brush, and wiping off all surplus with a piece of rag.
When dry, smooth down with a piece of canvas or coarse
rag, and fill up all nail-holes, etc., with stopping coloured
to match; then to gain the rich brown colour, wipe
over with a solution of ¼ lb. of asphaltum in 1 pt.
of turps. Allow this to stand till the next day to
harden, then varnish with church oak varnish of good
quality. (*g*) Should it be desired to imitate the figure
or grain of oak as well as the colour, satisfactory results
may be obtained by using size and yellow ochre instead
of umber. Pass a steel graining-comb over the asphaltum
when nearly set, and wipe clean a few light places with a
piece of rag slightly wet with turps and held in position
over the thumb of the right hand. The "sap" marks
will be concealed if they are coated at least twice
with the size and colour. In either case experiment on
a few odd pieces of similar wood previous to attempting
the actual work. (*h*) A much-admired orange-yellow
tone may be imparted to oak by rubbing it with a mixture
of about 3 ozs. of tallow and ¾ oz. of wax, with 1 pt. of
oil of turpentine. Mix by heating together and stirring.
This is used in a warm room, when the wood acquires
a dull polish. It is coated after an hour with thin polish,
repeating the coating of polish to improve the depth and
brilliancy of the tone.

Dark Oak.—(a) Take Vandyke brown ¼ lb., ammonia ¼ pt., and mix with water. (b) Mix 2 ozs. of pearlash and 2 ozs. American potash in a quart of hot water, and apply to the parts to be stained. (c) 2 ozs. Vandyke brown, 1 pt. liquid ammonia, 1 oz. bichromate of potash. A tinge of red in the potash or varnish will improve these. (d) Two pennyworth of Vandyke brown in oil, ¼ pint of terebine, ½ pint of turpentine, and ¼ pt. of kerosine or paraffin oil. Mix well, and try on a piece of planed deal, first laying it on thinly with a piece of sponge or old felt. If too dark, add more paraffin. This stain may be brightened by using more or less of raw sienna, also ground in oil, instead of all vandyke, thinning as required with paraffin oil. By some it is used largely for trade purposes, being cheap, easily and quickly applied, having a nice appearance, and leaving the work with a smooth surface ready for polishing or varnishing. (e) 4 ozs. American potash, 4 ozs. Vandyke brown. The potash must first be dissolved in a little water. Boil the brown in a gallon of water, and while hot add the potash. (f) A cheap substitute for dark oak stain can be obtained by thinning down with turpentine good Brunswick black to the shade required; but unless one thoroughly knows the nature of these materials, this plan had better not be adopted. Imitation antiques are thus treated, and finished by wax polishing.

Maple.—(a) Yellow pine, simply varnished with two or three coats of copal, or sized twice and varnished once, will be as near the tone of maple as can be got without painting and graining.

Mahogany.—(a) Common work, such as kitchen tables, chairs, etc., is generally wiped over with glue-size heavily stained with Venetian red; the desired tone being brought up by means of coloured polish and varnish. (b) For better class work it is better to wipe over first with a weak walnut stain, then a mahogany stain, which may be made by dissolving in water or spirits a little Bismarck brown. This is a very powerful pigment, and as much as will stand on a shilling will colour a

pint of polish probably sufficient for general use, though
more or less may be added according to the intensity
desired. Strain through muslin before using. (c) A
French plan is to first rub the surface with diluted
nitric acid, to prepare it for the materials subsequently
applied; it is afterwards treated with several applications of a filtered solution of 1½ oz. dragon's blood dissolved in 1 pt. methylated spirit, to which has been
added ½ oz. carbonate of soda. (d) A light brown
mahogany colour may be given by means of ⅓ lb. madder,
and ¼ lb. fustic, to 1 gal. of water applied hot. (e)
Boil ½ lb. of madder and 2 ozs. of logwood chips in 1 gal.
of water and brush well over the work while hot. When
dry, go over the whole with a solution of pearlash—
2 drachms to a quart of water. (f) Another cheap
mahogany stain is this: Put 2 ozs. of bruised dragon's
blood in a bottle with a quart of turpentine, and stand
in a warm place; shake frequently, and when dissolved
apply the mixture to the work. (g) To stain common
bay wood to resemble mahogany, wipe over with red
oil, made by soaking ¼ lb. alkanet root in 1 pt. of linseed
oil. Whilst still wet with oil, wipe over and well rub
in a weak solution of bichromate of potash (1 oz. to 1 pt.
of water); afterwards fill in, and use red polish. (h)
Wipe over with a weak walnut stain, and let this dry,
then use red oil and fill in, and polish with red polish.
(i) Water strongly impregnated with common lime,
washing soda, or carbonate of soda will give to common
mahogany tones varying from light Spanish to dark
rosewood. Any alkali will darken mahogany.

Rosewood.—(a) Stain first with a solution of 1 oz. extract of logwood, 1 qt. of water; put in the figure by the
aid of feathers or camel hair pencils dipped in copperas
solution or black stain; or add a little bichromate of
potash to the hot solution of logwood and grain with
that and a large feather cut so that it will make three or
four streaks at once. Rosewood grain can thus be easily
imitated. (b) First coat with mahogany stain; the
figure can then be put in with a small tuft of wadding

or a sponge dipped in black stain or black polish. (c) ¼ lb. cam-wood, 2 ozs. red sanders, 4 ozs. extract of log-wood, ½ oz. aquafortis, 1 qt. water. This gives a bright red ground. Put in the figure with copperas solution or black stain, and tone down with asphaltum dissolved in turps. (d) In a bottle mix ¼ lb. of extract of logwood, 1 oz. salts of tartar, and 1 pt. of water; in another bottle put 1 lb. of old iron in small pieces and 1 pt. of vinegar; after standing twenty-four hours it will be ready for use. To 1 pt. of varnish, add ¼ lb. of finely powdered rose-pink. Stain the wood with two coats of the logwood, allowing the first to become nearly dry before applying the second. A piece of rattan cane, sharpened at one end to a wedge shape and pounded so as to separate the fibres, will form a good brush. Dip this in the vinegar and with it form the grain, after which give the work a coat of the varnish and rose-pink. When staining, study the natural wood and imitate it as nearly as possible. The above materials skilfully applied to any common wood will make it re-semble rosewood so nearly that it will be difficult to dis-tinguish the difference. (e) Boil 1 lb. of logwood in 1 gal. of water, add a double handful of green walnut shells, boil the whole again, strain the liquor, and add to it 1 pt. of the best vinegar. It is then ready for use. Apply it boiling hot, and when the wood is dry, form red veins in imitation of the grain of rosewood with a brush dipped in the following solution : Nitric acid, 1 pt.; metallic tin, 1 oz.; sal-ammoniac, 1 oz. Mix, and set aside to dissolve, occasionally shaking.

Ebony.—(a) The usual method is to first coat the wood with a solution of 2 ozs. logwood extract, 1½ oz. copperas, 1 qt. water; add a dash of China blue or indigo; boil in an iron pot; apply hot; give several coats; then one or more coats of vinegar, in ½ pt. of which has been steeped 2 ozs. steel filings or rusty nails. (b) 1 gal. vinegar, 2 lbs. extract of logwood, ½ lb. green copperas, ¼ lb. China blue, 2 ozs. nut-galls. Boil in an iron pot till dissolved, then add ½ pt. iron solution made by steel filings and vinegar. (c) 8 ozs. gall-apple, 3 ozs. logwood extract, 2 ozs. vitriol, 2 ozs. verdigris, 1 gal. water, ½ pt. iron solution. (d) ½ lb. logwood, 3 qts. water, 1 oz. pearlash. Apply hot. Then take ½ lb. logwood, boil in 2 qts. water, add ½ oz. each of verdigris and copperas, and ⅓ pt. iron solution. These stains form a foundation only. The blackness is intensified by means of black "filling in" and the use of Frankfort black or gas black in the polish. (e) A recipe used by furniture manufacturers: Logwood chips, 8 ozs.; copperas, ½ oz. Boil the logwood in 1 gal. of water for half an hour, and add the copperas. Apply hot, giving two or three coats. In varnishing ebonised wood, a little black must be added or the varnish will give a brown shade. (f) To impart to pine, or any similar wood, a perfectly jet black surface, either bright or dull, mix some black with ordinary glue-size and apply to the wood. The mixture acts both as filling and stain. If the grain rises paper it down. When smoothing down any black wood, use a little linseed oil on the face of the glass-paper. For the polishing medium use white polish and gas black mixed, finishing off with clear polish without the black. But pine is not a good wood to ebonise. (g) The French black stain is sold by most veneer merchants, and gum merchants at 1s. per pint. It is not advisable to use it before polishing, as it contains free acid or salt, which is unfavourable for polishing and raises the grain. A suitable black stain for wood can be obtained at any oilman's. The ebony stains in general use are suitable for most woods. (h) For a very *lustrous* black, use black enamel upon a coating of flat black paint. A less brilliant surface would probably look the best, for which ebonise and then French polish.

The following recipes apply to darkening or improving the appearance of inferior woods :—

Fumigation.—This is the best method, though generally it is used only for oak and mahogany. Articles are given an appearance of age or enriched in colour by shutting them up for a time in an air-tight cupboard or box, on the bottom of which have been placed dishes of liquor ammonia ; ½ pt. is generally sufficient for a box 9 ft. long, 6 ft. high, 3 ft. 6 in. wide. It is a good plan to have a few squares of glass inserted, through which the action of the fumes can be watched. A well-made packing case will do, with strong brown paper pasted over the joints. This process will give shades varying from light olive to deep brown. Its chief advantage is that it does not raise the grain.

To test whether any kind of wood can be darkened by fumigation, take a piece freshly planed up on one side, take the stopper out of the ammonia bottle, and lay the wood over the mouth. The vapour of course will be strong, and if the wood can be darkened it will very soon show a patch of altered colour. A small bit of wood will do, anything large enough to cover the bottle's mouth. On a larger scale you can try by pouring some of the ammonia into a cup and covering the top in a similar way.

For fumigation to be effective, it is, of course, necessary for the woodwork to be perfectly free from grease or marks of handling. Should you be unable to procure a case large enough to hold the wood, a small spare room may be made to serve the purpose if the precaution is taken to paste paper over any openings such as the fireplace. Fumigated oak is generally finished by wax polishing, but there is no reason beyond custom why it may not be French polished or varnished. Some kinds of oak are not susceptible to ammonia vapour. It is not always convenient to adopt fumigation when a like result can be gained by other means.

Aniline dyes are useful for staining in self-colours, and these are generally used for decorative purposes, such as inlays. Fancy furniture and knick-knacks possess an individuality when thus treated, which is preferred to imitating any particular wood.

The following recipes are in general use, and apply to decorative and imitative treatment :—

Satin-wood. — 1 qt. spirits, 3 ozs. ground turmeric, 1½ oz. gamboge.

Rich Purple or Chocolate.—½ lb. madder, ¼ lb. fustic, ¼ lb. dragon's blood, 1 oz. common soda, dissolved in 3 pts. of spirits.

Purple.—1 lb. logwood chips, ¼ lb. pearlash, 2 ozs. indigo, 3 qts. water. Boil the logwood till the full strength is gained. Apply hot or cold.

Grey.—Maple may be stained a green-grey colour by using copperas in water or vinegar.

Green.—(*a*) A verdigris dissolved in hot vinegar, or the crystals of verdigris in hot water. A little indigo may be added, and two or three applications may be necessary. The proportions may be varied to obtain the desired tint. But the aniline dyes, as sold in packets or tubes for a few pence, will be found to meet all requirements, if only a small quantity—say a quart—is needed, especially if a little vinegar is added as directed. These dyes are often preferable, owing to the facilities for getting various shades. For instance, if the green is too bright, it is easy to add a little of the blue or black dye. It will be well to bear in mind that the hotter these stains are applied, the more deeply will they strike in. (*b*) Sponge the wood over with a decoction of turmeric, followed by one of Prussian blue.

Olive Green.—An olive-green colour, much in vogue in America for small tables, etc., is obtained by giving two coats of green stain and one of black; or the work might be stained green, and a black filling-in used.

Blue.—Indigo dissolved in dilute sulphuric acid, adding a little whiting to modify, or washing blue or China blue dissolved in vinegar.

Brown.—Vandyke brown ¼ lb., a pennyworth of burnt sienna, and 1 lb. of washing soda. Add 2 qt. of water and boil for twenty minutes. This stain costs only sixpence for 2 quarts, is very strong, and will stain in imitation of light oak, dark oak, or walnut, according to the number of coats that are applied.

Yellow.—(*a*) A great deal of the yellow finish on

wood is obtained by staining and sizing at one operation. Yellow ochre or lemon chrome is mixed with the patent or glue size. This is applied warm with a brush, the surplus being wiped off with a piece of rag. When dry, rub smooth with fine glasspaper, and finish with spirit or oil varnish. (*b*) Mix raw sienna with water and dissolve a little size in this mixture. Then, with a piece of sponge, take a portion of size and sienna, and rub it into the work to be stained until it is evenly coated, rubbing it nearly dry as you go. When dry, varnish with hard drying church oak varnish. (*c*) Apply a decoction of cochineal in water—say, 2 ozs. powdered cochineal boiled in 1¾ pt. of water for two and a half to three hours. When this is quite dry, go over the wood with a solution made up of 1¾ pt. of water in which 1 oz. of chloride of tin and ½ oz. of tartaric acid have been dissolved. (*d*) Another stain is made of turmeric dissolved in hot water or in methylated spirit. The colour can be varied by increasing or decreasing the quantity of turmeric. (*e*) Half an ounce of nitric acid diluted with 1½ oz. distilled or rain water. This will turn the wood yellow; if too dark, add more water. (*f*) The application of a decoction of yellow dyewood, or a solution of picric acid, or aniline yellow dissolved in varnish. (*g*) Dissolve common washing soda in boiling water, and add either yellow ochre or chrome yellow, whichever colour is preferred. (*h*) Barberry roots and twigs boiled in water will form a cheap yellow stain for wood when applied hot.

Cherry.—(*a*) Mix together, by stirring, 1 qt. of spirits of turpentine, 1 pt. of varnish, and 1 lb. of dry burnt sienna; apply with a brush, and after it has been on about five minutes wipe it off with rags. This stain takes about twelve hours to dry. (*b*) The following is a cheap cherry stain:—Take 3 ozs. of Bismarck brown, and dissolve in 1 gal. of boiling water. Add 1 gill of vinegar, to set the colour and prevent fading, and place away until cold, when it will be ready for use. (*c*) Another cherry stain is made by boiling 1 lb. of Spanish annatto in 1 gal. of water, to which has been added 1 oz. of concentrated (potash) ley. Evaporation over a gentle heat will give darker shades.

Many more recipes might be given, but any reader acquainted with the colour scale will readily perceive that a vast range of colour, or tones can be gained by combination. Quantities are omitted in several cases, for the simple reason that any convenient quantity can be used—if too strong, it is easy to add water; and it is worth while noting that curious effects are sometimes gained by spreading a stain of an entirely different colour over another. For instance, fancy tables stained a bright green have sometimes an over-glaze of black or blue.

Whatever the colour required, it is a good plan, and often saves much disappointment, if, before staining the work, a few similar pieces of wood are first experimented on till the required result is attained, bearing in mind that two rather weak applications are more effective than one strong one. The colouring is more evenly distributed, consequently a patchy appearance is avoided.

The practical French polisher does not aim at getting the exact tone by means of stains alone. He knows how far red oil, coloured filling in, dyed polish and varnish, etc., will aid him. The importance of this fact cannot be too strongly impressed upon readers; it may save much vexation when endeavouring to gain a particular result by means of stains alone.

In inlaid work the veneers are usually so carefully selected as to render any staining unnecessary. If, however, it must be done, protect the inlay by first giving it two or three coats of thin white hard varnish. This must be carefully done by means of a camel-hair pencil, allowing no varnish to spread on the portion to be stained; then use any stain desired. When dry, do the polishing with white or transparent polish, taking no notice of the varnish on the inlays till the first body of polish is on. Should the varnish then stand up in ridges above the polished portion, it can be levelled by means of fine glass-paper, on the face of which has been applied a little linseed oil.

The process required to stain veneers right through is called dyeing, but when the article is made and the surface of the veneer coloured afterwards the process is termed staining. For dyeing it is advisable to soak the veneer at least half a day in clean water; then take it out and allow a few hours to drain before inserting in the dye bath; this will cause the dye to penetrate more readily and be more evenly distributed. For staining purposes this is not necessary, as only the surface is acted upon.

Previous to staining woodwork from which the paint has been removed by lime process, rub it down with glass-paper, and coat the lime-burnt portion with vinegar; and when dry give it a good coat of warm glue or patent size; which will make the surface non-absorbent. Mix equal parts of varnish and turps, and stain with burnt amber in oil to the desired colour. For a more yellow colour use raw sienna for staining. Strain before using and spread carefully and evenly, brushing the way of the grain. When dry give another coating of stain if desirable, and finish with one or two coats of hard drying church oak varnish. Or when the paint has been cleaned right off the wood by lime, after vinegaring it can be stained with water satin; after this two coats of size and one of varnish should be applied. Any paint brush to suit the extent of surfaces will do, providing that it is quite free from dust or paint, and that the hairs don't come out in using.

CHAPTER XII.

PROCESSES OF VARNISHING WOOD.

AN idea more or less prevalent among those who do
not make the finishing of woods a business, is that
mahogany should generally be French polished, and that
other hard woods should either be polished in wax or
stained and varnished. These methods have their advantages, though they are not always the best to follow by
those who desire to finish some piece of woodwork quickly
and economically, and to produce a good result without
much trouble. For such work there is probably no
better method than that of using shellac varnish ; all
ordinary articles up to medium-priced furniture may be
finished in this way, provided that the wood is not
mahogany ; and even then it may be employed if the
operator cannot manage French polishing. The advantage of using shellac for a foundation in finishing all
kinds of wood, both soft and hard, is principally that it
produces an extremely hard surface when dry. As it
dries sufficiently hard in five or six hours to admit of
sand-papering, the work may be done expeditiously.
Moreover, shellac so effectually seals up the pores of
the wood, that when applied to the resinous timbers, it
even prevents the exudation of resin. Some years ago
furniture finishers used shellac on open-grained woods
without the filler, and this is done to some extent now ;
but experience has shown that the use of paste filler
is economical both in time and material.

To be successful in the use of spirit varnish it is
desirable that one should be somewhat acquainted with
the method of French polishing, for this gives, to a great
extent, the key to success. Unlike oil varnish, spirit
varnish, as a rule does not flow level after leaving the

brush. The beautiful level surface of oil varnish, as seen on carriage bodies, is gained by allowing the first coat to get perfectly dry, and then rubbing it down smooth by means of pumice in lump or in powder before applying the next coat.

The same principle underlies the successful use of spirit varnish. Each successive coat should be levelled by the aid of fine glass-paper or the polish-rubber; and it will further tend to success if, before any varnish is applied, the pores of the wood are sealed, either by the aid of a coat of size or by filling in and spreading over the work a few good rubbers full of polish. For small work the latter plan is recommended. Its object is twofold—it prevents the absorption of varnish by the unclosed pores of the wood, and keeps down the grain, which otherwise is apt to rise if no precautionary measures are taken.

A custom is now gaining in public favour of finishing many of the small knick-knacks and fancy articles of furniture with enamel paints, in preference to polishing or varnishing. This enamelling has much to recommend it, for apart from the pleasing variety thus gained by the use of artistic colours, and the fact that the articles can be made out of commoner, and consequently cheaper, woods, the enamel is easy of application, thus rendering it of service alike in the finishing of new goods and the renovation of old goods, in many cases giving the latter a new lease of life. The foundation of some of these enamels is spirit varnish, carefully mixed and blended with some dry pigment of the required shade. Before their use it is advisable to give new work a coat of size, but no other preparation is needed, not even levelling down by means of the polish-rubber. Moreover, some goods may be given a pleasing finish by thinning out the last coat by the addition of a little methylated spirit or linseed-oil, which will give a semi-lustrous or egg-shell finish that does not show up the inequalities of the woodwork to such prominence as a bright finish would.

Brushes for applying spirit varnish, whether clear or in the form of enamels, should be camel-hair of the kind known as gilders' mops (Fig. 11). These are strongly recommended, as the majority are far superior to those inserted in wood handles, whether round or flat. Those in tin should also be avoided unless they can be washed out in methylated spirit and put aside when not in use. For domestic purposes the varnish should be kept in a large-mouthed glass bottle, with the brush suspended from the cork (Fig. 12). This keeps it always at hand and in fit condition. Glass or earthenware

Fig. 11.—Gilder's Mop.

jars only should be used. Varnish containing shellac has a sort of corrosive action on tin, causing the varnish to turn dark-coloured and to smell disagreeably.

When only a small quantity of varnish is required, it is probable that the cost of gums, etc., would really cause it to be too expensive to make. Those who make a speciality of varnish making have the pick of the market, coupled with an extensive experience of the nature of the materials and requirements of their customers, and they can turn out a superior varnish, and in most cases can sell it at a less cost than it can be made at home.

Manufacturers claim that varnish should be used just as it is sold. While it is true that it is a mistake to add anything to the finer grades of varnish, the poor qualities are often too thick to work freely without diluting. If, therefore, it is necessary, add turpentine until the varnish spreads freely with a fitch. After varnishing, the work should be laid aside for at least twenty-four hours, by which time the coat will be hard, although if too much varnish has been used, it will be necessary to give the work more time before applying the next coat. A coat of varnish over one that is not perfectly hard will almost invariably result in "sweating," which will necessitate scraping the work and recommencing the job from the beginning; although if the sweating is only of a mild nature, an application of pumice-stone and water may remove it.

There are two varieties of shellac gum—orange and white. They may be bought dissolved in spirits of wine

Fig. 12.—Household Varnish Jar.

ready for use, and also dry in the shell-like lacs. If purchased in the lac, to prepare for use, dissolve 2½ lbs. of the white or 2 lbs. of the orange shellac in ½ gal. of spirits of wine. The white shellac costs more than the orange, but it produces a cleaner and neater job when it is desired to give a light finish. It is used for making transparent polish and varnish, such as that used on light-coloured goods and inlays. When bought it is not in flakes, like the orange, but is in the form of white twisted sticks, and being kept in stock under water, it

G

will naturally be damp. Therefore take the precaution
to crush the gum well, and spread it out in a warm room
to dry before adding the spirits. If the shellac solution
becomes too thick in consequence of the evaporation of
the spirit, it may be reduced to the required consistency
by adding more and agitating the mixture—preferably
in a warm place. Sometimes methylated spirit is used
instead of pure alcohol, but the smell is so objectionable
to those at work with it that it is not generally used in
first-class work.

The components of varnish vary, and the price
obtainable for the job, whether common or best work, is
an important factor in determining the quality. Shellac
generally forms the basis, and little else in the way of
materials can be used when really good work has to be
done. The addition of 2 ozs. of resin to a pint of French
polish makes a varnish that will suit for common work;
the addition of gum benzoin instead of resin will suit
for best work.

Varnish should always be applied in a warm room
free from dust. Varnished work is greatly improved by
the levelling-down process previously mentioned. For
this process the polish-rubber is required to be soft and
pliable, with rag covering, and a flat face free from
creases. When a coat of varnish is half dry—say, in
ten minutes—rub lightly in the way usual when French
polishing with the rubber charged with half polish and
half spirits, adding more spirits as required. It will
further tend to improve if, when rubbing down the last
coat, a few drops of glaze are added to the rubber.

When stained and thoroughly dry, the work is in a
condition to receive the first coat of varnish. It is of
importance that the work shall be in a perfectly dry
condition, and this can readily be ascertained by noticing
the uniformly dead appearance it presents, especially at
the corners and angles. All woods may have shellac for
a first coat of varnish. Birch, maple, and poplar may
readily be stained to imitate cherry, and require no
filling; but oak, ash, walnut. etc., are best treated with

a filler to close the pores of the wood. When all the filler has been thoroughly removed, clean the work down with cotton-waste, and it is then ready to receive the first coat of shellac. Where filling is not used, the shellac is applied after the work is sand-papered and stained.

The application of the shellac is often difficult to the beginner, although to the experienced hand it is perhaps the most pleasant part of the job, because its results are always the same. The object is to apply the shellac uniformly over the surface ; and this to an inexperienced hand is not easy, because the spirit evaporates quickly, and he is likely to go over the same ground twice, producing objectionable laps and unevenness.

If the work consists of panelling, the panels should be done first and the stiles and rails afterwards, finishing with the mouldings. The size of brushes used will depend upon the class of work under treatment, but comparatively small brushes will answer best in most cases. It is of importance to remember that the shellac must always be laid on with the grain of the wood, and when the brush is handled quickly and in a workmanlike manner the difficulties will not be great. It should also be borne in mind that the warmer a room is the quicker will the spirit evaporate and the coating of shellac harden.

After the coat of shellac has been on, say, six hours, it should be glass-papered to render the surface perfectly level. Use a thin glass-paper of a fine grade ; divide a sheet into four equal parts, and place the ends of a piece over the little finger and thumb. Rub fairly hard, but go very lightly over edges and mouldings, taking care not to cut through the varnish on protruding parts and edges. To reach corners, fold a piece of glass-paper into a triangle, moistening the paper if necessary. New glass-paper often scratches unevenly, and it is advisable to rub two pieces together to remove grit. Horsehair cloth may be used in very fine work instead of glass-paper. This can be obtained at any furniture repairing shop. Old cloth answers, and the hair side is used.

Having been thoroughly dusted off, the work is now ready for a second coat of shellac. This will be applied exactly in the same way as the first, and then, after glass-papering, it will be ready to receive the first coat of varnish. The varnishing done on this foundation may be of any quality, from cheap one-coat work up to a piano finish. If one coat only is to be used, a varnish should be employed that will dry with a good gloss. As a rule, two coats of varnish will be required, and the method of application will probably be the same whatever number of coats are given.

To apply varnish properly requires a good deal of practice, and it is impossible to lay down rules that shall govern the process. The inexperienced almost invariably apply too much varnish, the inevitable result being that the work cracks—an effect that destroys all pretensions to a good job. The following are given merely as hints : Dip the brush well into the varnish and lay it on *across* the grain, commencing at the least exposed portions of the work, so that in case it has to be handled the more prominent parts may not be marred. The varnish can should be provided with a wire or bar soldered across the middle of the mouth. Dip the brush as may be required, wipe it off on this bar, and lay off on the work as before. Stab the brush well into angles and corners. When the whole surface has been roughly covered, wipe the brush again on the bar, removing all the varnish possible ; then lay off the work with the grain of the wood, draw the brush backwards and forwards, and wipe it again if necessary. Repeat this operation until a perfectly level surface is obtained. If there are grooves or depressions in the work they will retain more varnish than the plain surface, and to prevent the surplus running down, the brush must be stabbed in and drawn out towards the main surface. It will be understood that the last coat of varnish introduced will make a very good job if the underneath coats of varnish and shellac respectively have been treated carefully in the manner described.

The process of rubbing down with pumice-stone is only applied when an extra fine finish is required, and in that case after the surface has been cleaned off the final operation of cleaning the work is proceeded with. Dip a small paint-brush in rubbing-oil thinned down with either petroleum or benzine (the finest grades obtainable should be used), and lightly paint over any mouldings, carvings, etc. Then go over the surface with a small cotton rag dipped in the oil, and rub off all with a dry rag, using also a clean brush to clean out the oil from the lines, carvings, etc.; and take care that all the oil is removed. Then take a soft rag moistened with alcohol, and go lightly over the whole work. As varnish will dissolve in alcohol, care must be taken to do this very lightly and quickly.

Where a fine finish is required, the best results are obtained by rubbing down each successive coat of varnish as it dries, and in that case a varnish that admits of rubbing must be used. When the first coat is thoroughly hard, take a piece of hair-cloth or worn sand-paper and lightly rub down the surface. Rub with the grain of the wood, and take care not to tear the varnish nor wear it through. Then clean the surface off thoroughly with the dusting-brush, and proceed to the second coat. Apply the second somewhat more heavily than the first coat, but take great care not to work up the under coat. The second coat will require thirty hours before a third is applied. If more than three coats are to be given, the thickness of each coat must be reduced accordingly. Between each coat of varnish a rubbing should be given as described, and for the best class of work the final coat may also be rubbed, but in a different manner. For this purpose a cotton or woollen rag is used, or a piece of felt. This is dipped into finely-powdered pumice-stone, and the rubbing is done lightly backwards and forwards with the grain of the wood. The most convenient plan is to keep the powdered pumice-stone in a small can or saucer with water added, and to pass the hand over the work during its progress,

to ascertain whether the surface is perfectly smooth.
Finally, the surface is thoroughly cleaned off with
sponge and water, and then well rubbed down with
a chamois leather.

Some classes of work need the final coats of varnish
to be polished. This is done as follows :—Take a little
powdered rotten-stone on a damp rag, and rub the work
lightly with the palm of the hand backwards and forwards, adding a little water if necessary, continuing the
rubbing until the surface is quite dry. The varnish will
present a very lustrous appearance, and then the work
may be cleaned off with petroleum. Drop ivory black
may be used with advantage instead of rotten-stone.
The work is often polished with the following wash
or its equivalent : raw linseed oil 1 qt., vinegar 1 pt.,
alcohol 1 pt., liquor ammonia ¼ pt.

Spirit varnishes are the only ones which properly
admit of being coloured. Often the resins themselves
will give the varnish a natural tint of yellow, brown, or
red ; in fact, pure colourless resin varnishes are only
obtainable by carefully selecting the materials for solutions, or by subjecting them to preliminary bleaching.
Of the resins which are most frequently used to
colour varnishes, dragon's blood and gamboge are the
principal. Dyewood extracts also play a considerable
part in the colouring of varnishes, and aniline dyes are
still more largely used. When shellac varnishes are
intended to be coloured with aniline, bleached lac only
should be employed. The aniline colour dissolved in
alcohol is added to the varnish after the latter has been
prepared, and the product should be warmed if necessary
to expel any excess of alcohol introduced with the aniline.
Picric acid gives a beautiful yellow colour, which may
be turned into a fine green by the addition of iodine
green. The two colouring materials in this case should
be added as separate solutions. A good blue colour may
be obtained with prussiate of iron free from alumina
and a green with acetate of copper. A mixture of
prussiate of iron with gamboge gives several good shades

of green, and with carmine or dragon's blood a violet. Coloured varnishes should be applied very quickly, in order to give a uniform tint. For application to polished surfaces, such as glass, wood, china, or metal, the addition of ½ per cent. of borax is an advantage.

Where varnishes and lacquers are required to be made by the aid of heat, or where large quantities are wanted, special plant and arrangements are necessary, but these cannot be treated of here. The following remarks apply to those varnishes and lacquers which can be made without the aid of heat, and where the quantity to be made at a time does not exceed the requirements of a moderate consumption. In making varnishes and lacquers of all kinds, care should be taken in every case to see that the spirit is of full strength, the resins free from moisture and all foreign matter; and where the finer sorts of varnishes are to be made, to see, also, that the resins are all picked. The resins should be small and, if possible, coarsely powdered, as large pieces take a long time to dissolve; while small pieces or powder get into a cohesive mass, in which state it is almost impossible to effect solution.

To effect speedy solution of the resins various plans are resorted to, such as constant agitation, with occasional immersion in hot water when the varnish or lacquer is being made in small quantity in a glass bottle, or by rolling jars or tins when the varnish is being made in quantities of two or three gallons, or by using casks turned by mechanical means where the required quantity is larger still. It may be convenient in the case of turpentine varnishes, which do not evaporate so quickly, to make them in wide-mouthed jars, and simply stir them frequently with a stick. If the stirring rod in this case is provided with cross-bars like the prongs of a dinner fork, the mass is more effectively broken up, and solution consequently hastened. It is almost unnecessary to say that the utmost care and cleanliness should be exercised in the making of varnishes, as the least dust or moisture will affect their quality.

It may be difficult to get methylated spirit of a strength ranging from 90 to 95 per cent., and pure alcohol is very expensive, so it may be well here to point out a ready plan for rectifying commercial methylated spirit in small quantity. Take a large bladder, which has been thoroughly freed from all fatty tissue both internally and externally, and fill it with methylated spirit 60 over proof, and hang it in a warm place. The water will ooze through the bladder and the spirit left inside will be correspondingly strengthened.

CHAPTER XIII.

VARNISHES.

SPIRIT varnishes are classified into groups as follows: —(a) Alcohol and sandarach; (b) alcohol and mastic; (c) alcohol and copal; (d) alcohol and amber; (e) alcohol and shellac; (f) alcohol and mixed resins.

These varnishes are very quick-drying, only less so than ether varnishes. They may be made to vary greatly in quality by the addition of essential oils, and are mostly colourless or only very slightly coloured. The addition of essential oils renders the varnishes more durable and elastic and less liable to crack through exposure to the air. These varnishes are largely employed in the bookbinding, leather and paper trades, and for certain kinds of metal-work, as well as for wood varnishes. In addition to sandarach, mastic, copal, amber, and shellac, other resins such as anime, elemi, benzoin, gamboge, and dragon's blood are frequently used in the preparation of these varnishes, the two latter specially as colourants, and camphor also is frequently incorporated.

Varnishes composed of spirit and shellac are among the oldest. Their natural red and yellow tints caused these preparations to become popular with furniture makers, and the introduction of bleached shellac completed the requirements of the trade by supplying a colourless preparation. Though shellac cannot be altogether dissolved in the spirits employed, yet a perfectly clear solution may generally be obtained by adding a little powdered lime and allowing it to settle. It then separates into two layers, the upper one (about three-fourths of the whole) being perfectly clear, and of the cloudy residue a part may also be rendered fit for use by filtration. A little petroleum or benzine may be used for clearing the solution, but in that case the cloudy layer rises to the surface, and none of it is recoverable by filtration.

Shellac may be dissolved with borax if 3 parts of shellac and 1 of borax are added to 25 parts of water, and the whole is moderately heated. The solution thus obtained is in itself an excellent varnish. It may be incorporated with oil colours by rubbing out these with a little oil, and then mixing with the varnish. The mixture dries within ten or fifteen minutes, and should be prepared only as required.

Brown spirit varnish is made of shellac, 2 lbs.; gum sandarach, $\frac{1}{2}$ lb.; methylated spirit (60 over-proof), 1 gal. Shake until the gums are dissolved, and add warmed Venice turpentine, $\frac{3}{4}$ lb. Shake until thoroughly mixed, and afterwards strain. It should be kept for a week or ten days previous to use.

Another spirit varnish is made of 4 ozs. shellac; 2 ozs. resin; $\frac{1}{2}$ oz. gum benzoin; $\frac{1}{2}$ oz. gum thus; 1 pt. methylated spirits. Crush the gums, pour in the spirits, and set aside in a warm place, frequently shaking the bottle. Carefully strain before using, and apply with a camel-hair brush.

White furniture varnish is made of bleached shellac, powdered, 2 ozs.; spirit, 1 pt. Dissolve the shellac in about two-thirds of the spirit, filter, then add first one-third of the remaining spirit, and afterwards dilute with the remainder. A reddish varnish may be made in the same manner by using orange instead of bleached lac, and a still darker one by the use of a very dark lac, with the addition of a little extract of sandal-wood.

Black varnish is made of thin orange shellac, 3 ozs.; spirit, 1 pint; Venice turpentine (previously liquefied), $\frac{3}{4}$ oz. Dissolve on water-bath, then add about $\frac{1}{2}$ oz. lamp-black.

Dark varnish is made of thin orange shellac, 3 ozs.; Venice turpentine, $\frac{1}{2}$ oz.; spirit, 1 pt. Dissolve the lac and turpentine in the alcohol on the water-bath.

The best white hard spirit varnish is made of fine picked gum sandarach, 2 lbs. Dissolve in methylated spirit, 1 gal. Strain and add finest pale turpentine varnish, 1 lb. Another dearer kind is made of gum mastic, 2¼ lbs.; stronger spirit, 1 gal. Dissolve, and add 1 lb. finest pale turpentine varnish.

Ether varnishes are classified into groups as follows : —(a) With pure ether basis ; (b) with mixed basis ; (c) with resin, chloroform, and benzine basis. These varnishes are generally of an exceedingly fluid character. They dry quickly, but they are not durable, and their application is therefore limited to objects which are not exposed to frequent cleaning or rubbing. The volatility of the solvents renders it necessary to keep ether varnishes in vessels very carefully closed. It is an advantage to give the articles to which these varnishes are to be applied a preliminary rubbing with oil of lavender or rosemary, after which they should be allowed to dry well before varnishing. The following is a recipe for an ether varnish.

Take of finely powdered copal, 3½ ozs.; ether (sp. gr. 0·725), 1 pt. Dissolve the copal in the ether in a stoppered bottle, constantly shaking ; if the copal is not entirely dissolved add a little more ether. Allow the solution to stand and settle, then decant into another bottle, and keep carefully stoppered.

A more quickly-drying varnish, specially suitable for small wooden articles, maps, etc., may be made by dissolving as explained above :—Finely powdered soft dammar, 5 ozs. ; in ether (sp. gr. 0·725), 1 pt.

A good varnish having a mixed ether solvent is made as follows :—Powdered mastic, sandarach, and glass, of each 2 ozs. ; ether (sp. gr. 0·725), ¼ pint ; alcohol, ½ pint ; lavender oil, 2 ozs. Mix the alcohol and the ether, and then add the resins and glass ; shake in stoppered bottle, allow to settle, and decant. The lavender to be added afterwards.

Another method of making ether varnishes is as follows :—Select the palest lumps of copal gum, crush them into small pieces and tie in a bag of fine muslin. Suspend this in a bottle of sulphuric ether, and the copal gum will gradually ooze out into the ether. When the gum has been digested, let the bag drain and then be put into another bottle of ether, which will dissolve all the available gum. Plenty of the gum should be used, so that the liquid will form a thick varnish. To make the varnish dry more slowly, and render it more elastic add any slow-drying essential oil, as oil of caraway, oil of anise, poppy, or sweet almonds ; these oils are colourless in small quantities. Should it dry too slowly, add more ether and mix thoroughly.

Varnish for gilded wood is made of sandarach, 1½ oz.; mastic in tears, 1½ oz. ; elemi, 1 oz.; spirit, 1 pt. The powdered resins are placed in a still with the alcohol and boiled for two hours. The product of distillation, about ½ pt., is collected. One third of this is replaced in the still and boiled for two hours more, after this the remaining two-thirds are placed in the still and similarly treated. The varnish thus obtained is very useful for protecting gilding, and allows the articles treated with it to be washed without injurious effect. The following are some useful formulæ of other varnishes for the same purpose made of powdered resins, dissolved in alcohol heated on a water-bath, turpentine being added if necessary :—(1) Mastic in tears, 3 ozs. ; sandarach 2 ozs. ; spirit, 1 pt. (2) Mastic in tears, 1½ ozs. ; sandarach, 1½ oz. ; shellac, 1 oz. ; colophony, 1 oz. ; spirit, 1 pt. A very hard and slow-drying varnish is made of : Mastic in tears, 2 ozs. ; sandarach, 2 ozs. ; copal, 1 oz. ; spirit, 1 pt. ; spike oil, 1½ oz. All these ingredients may be more or less varied. The varnishes may be perfumed with a few drops of any aromatic balsam.

Amber varnishes are usually prepared by first fusing the amber, then adding the other resins, next pouring the clarified linseed oil on the dissolved mass, and then diluting it with turpentine. Another way is to allow the amber to cool after dissolving and to repowder it and dissolve in the water-bath, together with the other resins in the oils. By exposing amber varnish to the sunlight the quality is improved.

Sandarach varnish is used for articles subject to friction and hard use, and may be applied to wood and even metals. The following formulæ will be found useful :— (1) Gum sandarach, 8 ozs.; pounded mastic, 2 ozs.; alcohol, 1 qt.; turpentine, 4 ozs.; pounded glass, 4 ozs. Mix and dissolve with frequent agitation. (2) Pounded copal of an amber colour once liquefied, 3 oz.; gum sandarach, 6 ozs.; mastic cleaned, 3 ozs.; clear turpentine, 2¾ ozs.; pounded glass, 4 ozs.; pure alcohol, 1 qt. Mix and dissolve with frequent agitation.

Bright varnish for toys and small wooden articles is made as follows :—Sandarach, 3 ozs.; copal, 1½ oz.; mastic, 1½ oz.; best turpentine, ¼ pt.; powdered glass, 2 ozs.; spirit, 1 pt. Dissolve on water-bath. A more durable bright varnish, for articles which have to stand wear, is prepared by dissolving on a water-bath :—Picked sandarach, 4½ ozs.; mastic in tears, 1 oz.; powdered glass, 2 ozs.; spirit, 1 pint. The varnish may be rendered more fluid by the addition of 8 ozs. of liquid Venice turpentine, after which it should be filtered. A very bright and quickly-drying varnish is made of sandarach, 1¾ oz.; mastic in tears, 1¾ oz.; copal, 1 oz.; oil of lavender, 1 oz.; spirit, 1 pt. Slightly damp the copal with oil of lavender and melt it in a well-glazed vessel on a slow fire, then run on a cold marble slab and powder. Add this powder to the powdered sandarach and mastic and dissolve on a water-bath in the alcohol. After solution add the lavender oil under stirring.

Perfumed varnishes are sometimes used, especially for imitation Chinese and Oriental articles. The following are formulæ for such preparations :—Dissolve on the water-bath powdered 1 lb. sticklac, ¼ lb. of picked benzoin, ¼ lb. of storax, and ½ lb. of sandarach in 5 pts. of spirit. Or prepare in the same way :—Shellac, 9 ozs.; mastic in tears, 4½ ozs.; picked benzoin, 2¼ ozs.; sandarach, 4½ ozs.; elemi, ½ oz.; myrrh, ½ oz.; amber, ½ oz.;

with 3 pts. of spirit ; and afterwards add, unde, stirring, ⅓ oz. of copaiba balsam, and filter.

Sealing-wax varnish for coating corks, etc., is made of good red sealing-wax, 3 lbs. ; shellac, 1 lb. Dissolve by agitation in 1 gal. methylated spirit. Black varnish may be made in the same way, and using the same proportions, substituting black for red sealing-wax.

Colourless varnish is made by dissolving with gentle heat 8 ozs. gum sandarach and 2 ozs. Venice turpentine in 32 ozs. alcohol. A harder varnish of a reddish tint is made by using 5 ozs. shellac and 1 oz. turpentine dissolved in 32 ozs. alcohol.

White varnish for maps, etc., is made of Canada balsam dissolved with a little less Venice turpentine and then strained.

Clear varnishes are made as follows, the parts being taken by weight :—(1) Linseed oil, 50 parts ; white lead, 2 parts ; litharge, 2 parts ; umber, 1 part. Add a little vermilion. (2) Linseed oil, 100 parts ; water, 50 parts ; litharge, 10 parts ; neutral acetate of lead, 1 part. Boil six or seven hours.

Essential oil varnishes are classified into groups as follows :—(a) Turpentine and mastic ; (b) turpentine and sandarach ; (c) turpentine and copal ; (d) turpentine and dammar ; (e) turpentine and various resins or mordants ; (f) mixed essential oils and resin. These differ in many important particulars from other classes of varnishes. The solvent does not entirely disappear during the drying processes of the varnish, but becomes incorporated in the hard surface layer. In practice the only essential oils used are turpentine, lavender, and rosemary, the two latter only in a minor degree. Turpentine to be used in varnish-making should always be well rectified and absolutely colourless. The boiling point of the oil is 160° C., so the manufacture of varnishes in which it forms an ingredient cannot be carried on at a very high temperature. Essential oil varnishes are notable for their fluidity, their brilliancy, and the quickness with which

they dry. Turpentine is by far the best vehicle for
dissolving resins. The incorporation of a fatty oil
into a turpentine varnish causes it to dry more slowly,
while it increases the hardness. Varnishes made with
essential oil only are used almost exclusively for indoor
work in house-painting, and for coating articles not
exposed to the open air, or which do not require
much handling or cleaning. Varnishes made with a
mixture of essential and fixed oils are mostly employed for outdoor work or other purposes where
there is generally much wear and friction. In preparing this class of varnishes, the resins may be
dissolved in cold oil, but, as this is a slow process,
they are generally dissolved separately under the
influence of heat, and should be allowed to cool.
The oil is then added slowly, constantly stirring.
The mixture is left to settle and then filtered.

Fat varnishes are slower in drying than many
others, but they are the most durable and hardest
of any. They are almost always used for outdoor
and other work requiring hard wear. In fat varnishes
almost all resins used in varnish-making can be incorporated, but copal and amber are those generally
used. The choice of the oil used as a solvent is of
prime importance. It should have been extracted
from properly-matured seed, cold-drawn oil being
generally better than that obtained by heat. It
should be thoroughly purified, limpid, of a pale
colour, and free from pungent odour. It is an advantage to use oil which has had time to settle
properly, and has been carefully drawn from the
receptacles in which it was stored.

Fat oil varnishes are classified in groups as follows :
—(a) Fixed oils and lead or zinc salts ; (b) fixed oils
and manganese salts ; (c) fixed oils and acids ; (d) fixed
oils and copal ; (e) fixed oils and amber ; (f) composite
fixed oil varnishes.

Linseed oil is the principal fatty oil employed in
the manufacture of oil varnishes. Varnish prepared

with it as the base should be as clear as water, of a pale straw colour, and of about 0·9575 sp. gr. It should, in drying, produce an even, colourless, and translucent coat. To cause the oil to dry it must be treated with metallic salts, preferably of lead, tin, or zinc. The metals are usually first granulated, zinc being used in the form of the sulphate of commerce, and should be calcined before use. The boiling of the metallic salts with the oil is done in a copper vessel in the proportion of 31 parts of oil to 1 each of tin and lead, and is continued until the salts are completely dissolved. The boiler is then taken from the fire and 2 parts of calcined and powdered zinc are added under vigorous stirring, producing effervescence. When this has subsided the mixture is again boiled for about half an hour, until bubbles cease. The varnish is then left to settle, and after twenty-four hours should be filtered through cloth. It is then bottled in vessels secured by a stopper sealed with lead, and exposed to the sun for seven or eight days to render it limpid. Litharge, minium, and white lead are also often used as oil driers, either combined or separately. The boiling is done on a naked fire or on the water-bath. Before boiling, a volume of water equal to that of the oil should be added to it to diminish the risk of taking fire, the metallic salts should, in this case, be placed in a copper-wire receptacle suspended in the upper layer of the liquid. The ordinary water-bath does not give a sufficiently high temperature for boiling the oil, but by using water saturated with sulphate of lime its boiling point may be raised. Take by weight: Linseed oil, 30 parts; water, 12 parts; litharge, 3 parts; white lead, 2 parts; umber, 1 part. Place the minerals in a cloth bag, suspend them in the oil, and boil until the water has diminished by one-eighth of its volume. Or take linseed oil, 100 parts; litharge, 9 parts; white lead, 7 parts; umber, 2 parts Mix the litharge with the oil, then add the umber and white lead by degrees when the oil begins to boil. Continue to boil for three or four hours.

The following tests for ascertaining the purity or otherwise of linseed oil have been collected. (1) Pure oil, at 15° C. (59° F.), has a specific gravity ranging between ·935 and ·932. Fish oil has a specific gravity almost the same. (2) Pure oil, boiled or raw, flashes at 244° C. (470° F.). Other fatty oils flash at about the same temperature. Resin oil flashes at between 149° and 165° C. (300° and 330° F.). The mineral oils used as adulterants flash at from 193° to 215° C. (380° to 420° F.). (3) When equal parts of linseed oil and nitric acid are put into a small white glass bottle and shaken up, the mixture will appear, after standing for fifteen minutes or so, when the oil used is pure linseed, as an upper layer of muddy olive-green and a lower one almost colourless ; when fish oil is present, the upper layer will be a deep red-brown and the lower layer a deep blood-red. (4) Shaken up with soda and then having some warm water added, if any petroleum is present, it will separate from the emulsion. (5) When put in a bottle and buried in a mixture of ice and salt, cottonseed oil will solidify ; pure linseed oil remains liquid till 17° F. is reached.

Varnish for musical instruments must be extremely pliable, and it must adhere to the wood without cracking and without thickening in crevices, thus forming an obstacle to the proper use of the instrument. For this reason shellac and oily bodies are inadmissible. Varnishes for musical instruments are generally coloured red or yellow, but the colouring materials should not in this case be prepared by the usual mode of alcoholic solution, but by distilling the varnish on a water-bath at a temperature of about 100° C., in which case the alcohol evaporates (its point of distillation being about 78°), while the essential oil remains behind. The following are suitable recipes. (1) Sandarach, 1½ oz.; mastic in tears, 2 ozs.; elemi, ½ oz.; turpentine, ½ oz.; castor oil, ½ oz.; spirit, 1 oz. (2) Mastic in tears, ¼ oz.; soft white dammar, ¼ oz.; turpentine, 2 ozs.; raw linseed oil, ¼ oz. Put the turpentine in a broad-bottomed bottle,

H

with a small quantity of powdered glass, and add the mastic. Stir frequently, and after twenty-four hours add the dammar. Leave to stand for another twenty-four hours, and then add the linseed oil while stirring. Let the mixture stand for a fortnight in strong light; then filter through cotton. This varnish improves with age, and is best when six or eight months old.

Varnishes, in which the solvent consists of a mixture of an essential oil and linseed oil, do not dry so quickly as pure turpentine varnishes, but they are much harder and more durable, and are largely used for outside work by carriage-builders, etc. Shellac, by reason of its insolubility in fixed oil, is rarely employed in these varnishes, its place being generally taken by copal or amber. The following are some recipes for varnishes of this class :—Varnish for distempering paint.—Dissolve on the water-bath with a little turpentine : Powdered mastic, ½ oz.; powdered white olibanum, 1 oz. Add to the mixture while hot : Venice turpentine, 1 oz.; plain oil varnish, ½ oz.; turpentine, 1 pt. Carriage varnish. — Hard copal, 5 ozs.; plain oil varnish, 1 pt.; turpentine, 1 pt.

Varnishes which consist of all those preparations which include beeswax, and which are used as furniture polishes are fully treated upon in Chapter VI.

The dulling or blooming which sometimes mars the appearance of a varnished surface is caused by the presence of water. Gelatine is insoluble in spirit, and a thin sheet of gelatine cut in strips and put in the varnish will absorb the water and make the varnish as good as ever, so that it can be used clear and bright to the last drop. When the strips of gelatine become quite soft, through absorbing the moisture, they may be taken out and dried, and are then ready for use again.

To refine shellac 1½ lb. of soda are dissolved in 45 lbs. of water in a suitable boiler. Add to this gradually as it dissolves 5 lbs. of shellac. This forms a solution of violet-red colour, with more or less trace of fatty substances. After complete solution the mixture is boiled for a few minutes, and the boiler is then covered with a wooden top, which is cemented down, and the contents of the boiler are cooled slowly. When cold, the grease on the surface of the solution is skimmed off, and, by means of sulphuric acid added drop by drop, the shellac is precipitated, and well washed with water until all acid reaction is removed. The shellac is then put into boiling water and softened, so that it may be worked into rods or plaits, and is hardened by transferring it to cold water containing some glycerine. The refined shellac should have a silver to a yellowish-white surface, with a yellowish-brown fracture. It should be perfectly dry and entirely soluble in alcohol. The turbidity of alcoholic solutions of shellac is caused by a fatty substance present to the extent of 1 to 5 per cent. To remove this, add 1 part of powdered chalk, and heat to 112° F. The greater portion of the solution clears rapidly, and the remainder may be clarified by filtering once.

Spirit and copal varnishes should be prepared with pieces of transparent copal as nearly as possible of the same tint. Gum copal, although difficult of solution in lumps, has the property of liquefying when reduced to very fine powder and kept exposed to a current of air. There is a great variety of copals, but for general purposes they may be divided into hard, half hard, and soft copals. The preparation of copal varnishes was formerly a difficult and arduous work, no easy process being known for completely dissolving the copal. But these difficulties have been overcome by the system of dissolving it on the water-bath, at a temperature of about 100°, in as much spirit as is required to give the necessary fluidity to the varnish, or by that of treating both the resin and the solvent in a closed vessel at a temperature of about 300°. Half-soft copal contains more moisture than the hard resin, and dissolves quicker. If over heated it may turn black and be spoilt altogether. Care should also be taken to dilute it with turpentine as soon as the oil has been incorporated. The following makes a useful varnish :—Half-soft copal, 1¼ lb. ; boiled linseed oil, ¼ to ⅓ pt., turpentine, 1 gal.

For quick-drying copal varnish the following are two formulæ :—(1) Turpentine, 1 pt. ; spirit, ½ pt. Mix, and whilst slowly stirring, add powdered copal, 4 ozs. Dissolve at about 100° on the water-bath, leave to settle, and decant. (2) Powdered copal, 18 ozs. ; turpentine, 3 pts. ; copaiba balsam, 3 ozs. ; spirit, 1 pt. Prepare in the same manner.

Fat copal varnish requires a good deal of skill in its preparation, especially in the manipulation of the copal solution, which is easily spoilt by insufficient or excessive heat. Great care should be taken to select copal of the same colour and the same degree of hardness. The oil should be added to the copal as soon as most of the largest pieces have dissolved. Exceptionally hard pieces which may remain undissolved should be taken out and collected to make a special solution. The oil before being poured on to the copal should be heated to about the same temperature, but it must not be added in a boiling state. The following proportions are usual :—Hard or half-soft copal, 1 part ; oil, 9 parts ; turpentine, slightly over 2 parts. The oil should be added slowly ; to incorporate itself properly with the copal, it should be between 120° and 150°. If too hot, effervescence will take place, if too cold it will form a cakey varnish.

Copal varnishes are also made by the cold process, but the solution of copal in essential oil generally offers certain difficulties, especially when heat is used. The following process seems well adapted for obtaining copal varnish without the use of heat :—Reduce the copal to powder and then add gradually the spike oil or other essential oil solvent, beating up the two vigorously in a mixer. Gradually the copal dissolves, and the solution may be filtered. If turpentine is afterwards added to copal dissolved in the cold way in spike oil, the copal is precipitated, which does not occur if solution has been effected by the aid of heat. A mixture of 1 part of spike oil to 9 parts of turpentine may be added to the copal without causing precipitation, and will produce a good varnish. By mixing powdered copal with spike oil and then mixing linseed-oil with the product, a uniform mixture is also obtainable. Dammar resin is rather more soluble than copal in essential oil, but in using this or, any kind of soft resin, it should either be dissolved over a naked fire previous to being mixed with the solvent, or the latter should be added boiling. This is done because soft resins contain a considerable proportion of water, and, unless previously dried, are apt to spoil the varnish. Take powdered dammar, ¾ lb., and form a thick solution with about ½ pt. of turpentine, put the mixture on the fire and when it commences to boil remove from the fire and, under constant stirring, add ¼ to ½ pt. of turpentine, bring the mixture on the fire again and heat to boiling point ; then withdraw, allow to stand, and filter. The addition of about ¼ oz. of camphor will facilitate the solution.

Hard copal varnish is made by dissolving on a naked fire 4 ozs. of hard copal, and adding slowly fully 1 pt. of oil, heated to 150°. Then add about 1¼ pt. of turpentine, filter, and keep in closed vessels. The addition of oil of rosemary during the heating of the copal will give a colourless varnish at a comparatively low temperature. Hard copal, 1 oz.; rosemary oil, ¼ oz.; linseed oil, ¼ pt.; turpentine, ¼ pt. The linseed oil may be replaced by copaiba balsam, thus : Dissolve 3 ozs. of hard copal, add 1 oz. of heated copaiba ; dilute with 1 pt. of turpentine.

CHAPTER XIV

REPOLISHING SHOP-FRONTS.

IT is assumed that only those who have some knowledge of the craft, and skill in manipulations will care to undertake the job of repolishing a shop-front, which is so freely exposed to the criticism of every passer-by. It is not necessary to enter into general details, as these have been already dealt with. A grain-filler need not be used on work that has been previously polished ; the polish-rubber should be kept soft and pliable, to enable it to get into the quirks, corners, and carvings ; the best of materials only should be used ; oil should be sparingly applied ; spirit is to be preferred to glaze, and co ensure the work standing out bright and bearing future inspection, the varnish used should have but a small percentage of resin. When the varnish is bought ready made, that known as " best brown hard " should be procured ; mix it with an equal bulk of polish before applying it to the work.

To polish or repolish a shop-front with a mahogany swing-door, and, perhaps, a vestibule, is a more difficult task than polishing household furniture in the workshop or at the bench. If the woodwork is all new, it will present no difficulties to a practical polisher, provided the day is warm and bright and free from excessive damp or moisture. Then methylated spirit can be used as a solvent for the shellac, and the work will stand out bright. Damp or excessive cold will cause the polished work to chill or turn white, and then it will be advisable to use wood-naphtha in place of spirits, working each rubber fairly dry, and avoiding the use of spirit varnish as much as possible.

In repolishing, cleanliness is most important ; for it will be found that more satisfaction is given if the woodwork is clean, and of an even colour, than if a heavy body of polish is laid on an uncleaned surface which has the dirt clinging in the corners, quirks, and carvings. Careful attention to this detail stamps a polisher as a good workman, and enables him truthfully to print on his trade-card : " Old work repolished equal to new."

Unfortunately, shop-fronts are generally allowed to get into a very bad state before it is decided to incur the expense of repolishing. The polish becomes worn off the bottom rail, which is black and dirt-begrimed ; the lower part of the pillars is light in colour ; the door has faded on the lower half, and the upper portion has only been kept from reaching the same condition by the covering of dirt which intercepts the sunlight. In such a case, the best plan would be to scrape off all the polish, smooth down with glass-paper, wiping the work over with " red oil," and allow it to stand the night To make the red oil, steep ¼ lb. alkanet root in 1 pt. raw linseed oil. It imparts to mahogany a rich colour if allowed to stand at least twelve hours, in sunshine if possible. This work may be said to belong more properly to the shop-fitter, and would practically mean placing the job in the polisher's hands as new work.

This method may be deemed too expensive, and in that case we must content ourselves with gaining a clean surface by washing it down with strong soda water —½ lb. common washing soda to 1 gal. warm water— assisted by a little powdered pumice stone or bath-brick, and using a scrubbing-brush to get the dirt out of the corners, quirks, carvings, etc., afterwards swilling off with clean water and wiping dry. Should the dirt still remain and leave the corners, etc., dark in colour, it may be necessary to bleach these. This is done by brushing over with weak solution of oxalic acid—½ oz. to 1 pt. warm water—and swilling off again with clean water. The bleached portions, when dry, must be wiped over with common malt vinegar to kill any trace of the acid, and thus prevent its eating through the polish.

Now it will be possible to see exactly how the work stands. Any very light portion, if covered with a good body of polish, should have this polish removed by rubbing with No. 1 glass-paper, on the face of which a little methylated spirit has been sprinkled. Then all nail-holes and cracks should be stopped with putty, coloured to match by mixing some Venetian red, or, better still, with beeswax and resin in equal parts, coloured by the same means as the putty, and pressed in whilst hot with a piece of stick.

After smoothing down the surface with worn glass-paper, and wiping free from dust, the work should be wiped all over with a rag moistened with linseed oil, to enable the new polish to take more kindly to the old, and all bare portions and light-coloured places should be bodied-up with coloured polish to equalise the shade. The whole of the work may then be treated, still using polish with a little colour in to make it look more lively. Bismarck brown is generally used as the colouring medium, but it is not always advisable to use it for out-door work, except when the work is merely bodied-up with it, and finished with a clear polish.

The sun's action has a great influence on these brilliant reds; if exposed to the glare of sunlight they will soon fade unless protected. It is preferable to use red sanders, though it does not look so powerful when seen in the bottle. Two ounces of this steeped in a pint of polish, and carefully strained before using, will be found satisfactory. When well worked with the rubber, it will be found to gain in intensity and to enrich the work and more closely imitate the colour of mahogany than does the Bismarck brown, which gives the more glaring red often seen on common furniture.

Though the instructions here given are for mahogany work, they apply equally to walnut, except that the red added to the polish must not be so intense.

Black work should be cleansed in the same manner as described above, and the polishing done with black polish. This can be bought as ebonite, ready made, or combined ebony stain and polish may be used, or it can be made by dissolving 4 ozs. garnet shellac in 1 pt. spirit. Its blackness will be intensified by adding 1 oz. of black aniline dye. The white polish as made from bleached shellac may be used instead if similarly dyed. The black aniline dye soluble in spirit, which can be obtained at most shops where polishers' sundries are sold is the proper kind for this purpose. Should any great difficulty arise, gas black is a useful substitute. Where there is any incised work to be gilded, finish the polishing before this is attempted.

It is sometimes necessary to remove paint from shop-fronts that have been painted on an ebonised or polished ground. The following method was adopted in a case where some mahogany shop-fronts that had been painted were required to be polished in their natural colour. Burning off was out of the question, owing to the glass and the liability to scorch the wood. One bucketful of a strong solution of freshly slaked lime, to which was added about 2 lbs. common soda, 1 lb. soft soap, ¼ pt. liquid ammonia, was used. This, laid on with an old brush, soon softened the paint, and enabled it to be scraped off with a chisel-shaped putty knife and steel scrapers. Many applications were required, and several brushes were soon spoilt by the corrosive action of the solution; but eventually all the paint and polish was removed. The work was then bleached with oxalic acid, vinegared, red-oiled, and lastly polished with coloured polish; and after two years' wear the job will still bear inspection. Some difficulty occurred in removing the paint from all the quirks; these, and other portions which showed themselves dark in the polishing, were touched up with Venetian red mixed in 1 part polish and 3 parts spirit, and when dry these portions were coated with red varnish and polished.

It is necessary to know how to remove the polish and varnish from the glass, because, however careful one may be in polishing, varnish is sure to get on the glass;

indeed, to ensure that the pillars, etc., have an even body on, and look well to the extreme edges, it is desirable *not* to study the glass. The polish can be removed when all is hard and dry by taking a sponge, wet with clean water, wiping it over the glass and polish, etc., and, whilst wet, cutting upwards with a sharp ¾-in. or 1-in. carpenter's chisel. If care is taken to keep the glass wet and the chisel sharp, there will be no danger of scratching the glass.

The following recipes may be useful in polishing shop-fronts : — *French Polish* — Dissolve 4 ozs. best orange shellac in 1 pt. methylated spirit. *Spirit Varnish* — Shellac, 3 ozs. ; gum sandarach, 3 ozs. ; mastic, ¼ oz. ; Venice turpentine, 1 oz. ; camphor, 10 grs. ; spirit, 20 ozs. *Red Oil*—Alkanet root, ¼ lb. steeped in 1 pt. raw linseed oil. *Red Stain*—½ oz. Bismarck brown dissolved in ½ pt. spirit ; a few drops to be added to the polish or varnish, to make what is commonly termed red polish or red varnish.

INDEX.

PRINTED BY CASSELL & COMPANY, LIMITED, LA BELLE SAUVAGE, LONDON, E.C.
50. 504

Electro-Plating. With Numerous Engravings and Diagrams.

Contents.—Introduction. Tanks, Vats, and other Apparatus. Batteries, Dynamos, and Electrical Accessories. Appliances for Preparing and Finishing Work. Silver-Plating, Copper-Plating. Gold-Plating. Nickel-Plating and Cycle-Plating. Finishing Electro-Plated Goods. Electro-Plating with Various Metals and Alloys. Index.

Clay Modelling and Plaster Casting. With 153 Engravings and Diagrams.

Contents.—Introduction. Drawing for Modellers. Tools and Material for Modelling. Clay Modelling. Modelling Ornament. Modelling the Human Figure. Waste-moulding Process for Plaster Casting. Piece-moulding and Gelatine Moulding. Taking Casts from Nature. Clay Squeezing or Clay Moulding. Finishing Plaster Casts. Picture Frame in Plaster. Index.

Violins and Other Stringed Instruments. With about 180 Illustrations.

Contents.—Materials and Tools for Violin Making. Violin Moulds. Violin Making. Varnishing and Finishing Violins. Double Bass and a Violoncello. Japanese One-string Violin. Mandolin Making. Guitar Making. Banjo Making. Zither Making. Dulcimer Making. Index.

Glass Writing, Embossing, and Fascia Work. (Including the Making and Fixing of Wood Letters and Illuminated Signs.) With 129 Illustrations.

Contents.—Plain Lettering and Simple Tablets. Gold Lettering. Blocked Letters. Stencil Cutting. Gold Etching. Embossing. French or Treble Embossing. Incised Fascias, Stall-plates, and Grained Background. Letters in Perspective; Spacing Letters. Arrangement of Wording and Colors. Wood Letters. Illuminated Signs. Temporary Signs for Windows. Imitation Inlaid Signs. Imitation Mosaic Signs. Specimen Alphabets. Index.

Other Volumes in Preparation.

DAVID McKAY, Publisher, 610 South Washington Square, Philadelphia.

TECHNICAL INSTRUCTION.

Important New Series of Practical Volumes. Edited by PAUL N. HASLUCK. With numerous Illustrations in the Text. Each book contains about 160 pages, crown 8vo. Cloth, $1.00 each, postpaid.

Practical Draughtsmen's Work. With 226 Illustrations.
Contents.—Drawing Boards. Paper and Mounting. Draughtsmen's Instruments. Drawing Straight Lines. Drawing Circular Lines. Elliptical Curves. Projection. Back Lining Drawings. Scale Drawings and Maps. Colouring Drawings. Making a Drawing. Index.

Practical Gasfitting. With 120 Illustrations.
Contents.—How Coal Gas is Made. Coal Gas from the Retort to the Gas Holder. Gas Supply from Gas Holder to Meter. Laying the Gas Pipe in the House. Gas Meters. Gas Burners. Incandescent Lights. Gas Fittings in Workshops and Theatres. Gas Fittings for Festival Illuminations. Gas Fires and Cooking Stoves. Index.

Practical Staircase Joinery. With 215 Illustrations.
Contents.—Introduction : Explanation of Terms. Simple Form of Staircase —Housed String Stair : Measuring, Planning, and Setting Out. Two-flight Staircase. Staircase with Winders at Bottom. Staircase with Winders at Top and Bottom. Staircase with Half-space of Winders. Staircase over an Oblique Plan. Staircase with Open or Cut Strings. Cut String Staircase with Brackets. Open String Staircase with Bull nose Step. Geometrical Staircases. Winding Staircases. Ships' Staircases. Index.

Practical Metal Plate Work. With 247 Illustrations.
Contents.—Materials used in Metal Plate Work. Geometrical Construction of Plane Figures. Geometrical Construction and Development of Solid Figures. Tools and Appliances used in Metal Plate Work. Soldering and Brazing. Tinning. Re-tinning and Galvanising. Examples of Practical Metal Plate Work. Examples of Practical Pattern Drawing. Index.

Practical Graining and Marbling. With 79 Illustrations.
Contents.—Graining: Introduction, Tools, and Mechanical Aids. Graining Grounds and Graining Colors. Oak Graining in Oil. Oak Graining in Spirit and Water Colours. Pollard Oak and Knotted Oak Graining. Maple Graining. Mahogany and Pitch-pine Graining. Walnut Graining. Fancy Wood Graining. Furniture Graining Imitating Woods by Staining. Imitating Inlaid Woods. Marbling ; Introduction, Tools, and Materials. Imitating Varieties of Marble. Index.

Painters' Oils Colors and Varnishes. With Numerous Illustrations.
Contents.—Painters' Oils. Color and Pigments. White Pigments. Blue Pigments. Chrome Pigments. Lake Pigments. Green Pigments. Red Pigments. Brown and Black Pigments. Yellow and Orange Pigments Bronze Colors. Driers. Paint Grinding and Mixing. Gums, Oils, and Solvents for Varnishes Varnish Manufacture. Index.

Practical Plumbers' Work. With 298 Illustrations.
Contents.—Materials and Tools Used. Solder and How to Make It. Sheet Lead Working. Pipe Bending. Pipe Jointing. Lead Burning. Lead-Work on Roofs. Index.

Practical Pattern Making. With 295 Illustrations
Contents.—Foundry Patterns and Foundry Practice. Jointing-up Patterns. Finishing Patterns. Circular Patterns. Making Core Boxes. Boring Holes in Castings. Patterns and Moulds for Iron Columns. Steam Engine Cylinder Patterns and Core Boxes. Worm Wheel Pattern. Lathe Bed Patterns. Head Stock and Poppet Patterns. Slide-rest Patterns. Valve Patterns and Core Boxes. Index.

DAVID McKAY, Publisher, 610 South Washington Square, Philadelphia.